Shaka

## JACANA POCKET SERIES

The new series of Jacana pocket guides is meant for those who are looking for a brief but lively introduction to a wide range of topics of South African history, politics and biography, written by some of the leading experts in their fields.

*Already published*

Steve Biko
(by Lindy Wilson)
Shaka
(by Dan Wylie)

Umkhonto weSizwe
(by Janet Cherry)
San Rock Art
(by J.D. Lewis-Williams)

*Forthcoming titles*

The ANC
Marxism in South Africa
Liberalism in South Africa
A history of epidemics
A history of the Zulu
The TRC
South Africa & WWII

Govan Mbeki
Eugène Marais
Ingrid Jonker
Albert Luthuli
Mohandas Gandhi
H.F. Verwoerd
Olive Schreiner

# Shaka

A Jacana Pocket Biography

Dan Wylie

First published by Jacana Media (Pty) Ltd in 2011
10 Orange Street
Sunnyside
Auckland Park 2092
South Africa
+2711 628 3200
www.jacana.co.za

© Dan Wylie, 2011

All rights reserved.

ISBN 978-1-77009-962-3

Set in Minion 10.5/15pt

Printed and bound by Ultra Litho (Pty) Limited, Johannesburg

Cover by Joey Hi-Fi

Job No. 001396

See a complete list of Jacana titles at www.jacana.co.za

# Contents

Introduction . . . . . . . . . . . . . . . . . . . . . . . . . . . . . . . 7

1 Who do we trust? The problem of sources . . . . . . 14

2 He was not alone: Shaka in context . . . . . . . . . . . 27

3 Beetle or axe? Ancestry, birth and childhood . . . . 39

4 Learning the craft: Shaka comes to power,
   c. 1800–1812 . . . . . . . . . . . . . . . . . . . . . . . . . . . . . 49

5 The bulls of the herd: Shaka and the north,
   1812–1824 . . . . . . . . . . . . . . . . . . . . . . . . . . . . . . . 59

6 The limits of control: Shaka and the south,
   1812–1824 . . . . . . . . . . . . . . . . . . . . . . . . . . . . . . . 69

7 The nature of the state . . . . . . . . . . . . . . . . . . . . . 81

8 The nature of the man . . . . . . . . . . . . . . . . . . . . . 95

9 Black in all other respects: Shaka and the white
   visitors, 1824–1828 . . . . . . . . . . . . . . . . . . . . . . . 109

10 Red assegais: The final phase, 1824–1828 . . . . . 122

11 Aftermaths . . . . . . . . . . . . . . . . . . . . . . . . . . . . . 138

Further reading . . . . . . . . . . . . . . . . . . . . . . . . . . . 149

Index . . . . . . . . . . . . . . . . . . . . . . . . . . . . . . . . . . 153

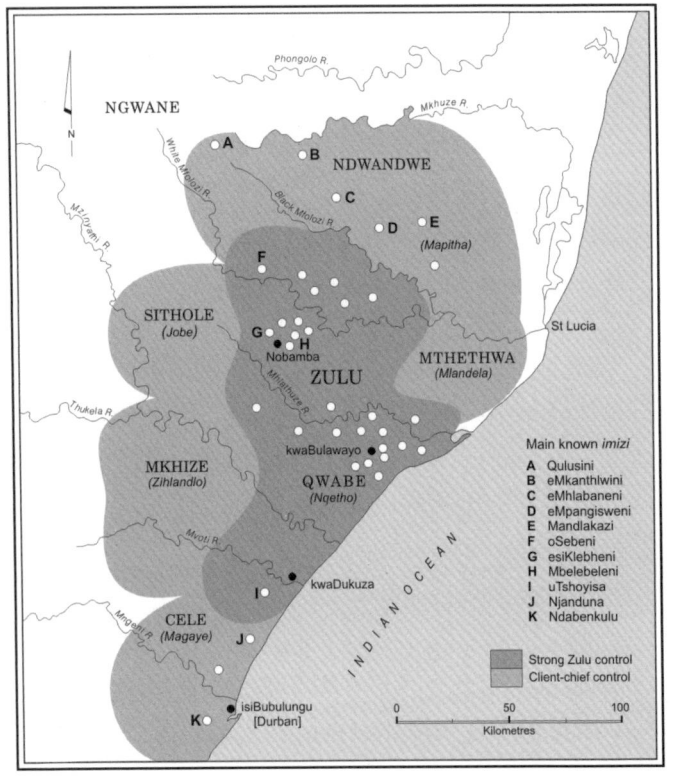

*The Zulu polity under Shaka, c. 1825.*

# Introduction

Shaka is a household name. One can scarcely utter the word 'Zulu' without the picture of the great founder-king coming to mind. For hundreds of thousands of television viewers across the globe, that picture will actually be the whipcord-muscled, snarling image of Henry Cele, the football player who acted Shaka in Bill Faure's 1986 series, *Shaka Zulu.* A Cele-like statue of Shaka, towering beneath an extravagant blue crane feather, symbol of kingship, dominates the entrance to the former provincial parliament at Ulundi in KwaZulu-Natal. Not far away, 'Shakaland', a converted Faure film set, seduces thousands of tourists every year into believing they are experiencing the 'real Zulu'. A little further south, in Durban, one can now find another playground for the wealthy, the uShaka Marine World, an anchored corvette and a controversial new airport, all named after him. And much more.

The landscape of literature, too, bristles with legends

*Bill Faure's 1986 epic television series,* Shaka Zulu, *was both politically controversial and wildly popular, at least outside South Africa. Shaka's image is now irretrievably associated with the lead actor, the late Henry Cele. (Courtesy of the SABC)*

of the heroism and sadism, the genius and madness, of Shaka. In Elizabeth Paris Watt's 1948 novel, *Febana*, he is a Satanic mass-murderer. In the once-president of Senegal Léopold Sédar Senghor's play-for-voices, *Shaka*, he is a rallying symbol across the continent for African liberation from colonial oppression. He is the subject of a new opera by J S Mzilikazi Khumalo. The bookshelves of thousands of households carry E A Ritter's oft-reprinted book *Shaka Zulu*, the 1955 novel which has been widely, but misguidedly, accepted as accurate history.

But most of what we have been told about Shaka over the last century and a half is simply wrong. A massive machinery of politically motivated myth-building, outright lies, culturally biased misconceptions, sloppy scholarship and unthinking repetition has created a historiographical Frankenstein's monster: a grotesquely distorted image patched together from ill-informed fictions and gothic speculations, for almost all of which there is simply no evidence.

One of the myth's latest manifestations appears in a chapter of Max du Preez's book *Of Warriors, Lovers and Prophets*. 'History will never be the same,' the back cover trumpets. Unhappily, in this case one of South Africa's most admired investigative journalists has done almost no investigating at all. Like so many of his 'historian' predecessors, Du Preez simply repeats the most ill-conceived of Shaka tales, selecting the sensational bits from a single eyewitness account and, mostly, E A Ritter – the illegitimacy, the pathological murderousness, the sexual perversity, his love for 'Pampata' (who, unfortunately for Du Preez, did not exist). Sweeping aside all recent scholarship, Du Preez encapsulates the picture of Shaka that has become familiar to most of us: 'the genius militarist who rose from humble beginnings to forge a nation and change the history of an entire sub-continent'. But what is the actual evidence for that 'genius'? What was the real nature of this instantaneously forged 'nation'? An 'entire sub-continent'? Hang on a bit. When we observe Du Preez recycling the usual exaggerated figures – 7000 killed here, whole regiments there – for which there is no credible documentation, we know we are once again wallowing in the realm of myth and speculation.

Du Preez's chapter is only one example of the salacious, shallow and uncritical tale-telling that began, effectively, in 1836, with the very first publication by an eyewitness of Shaka's reign, Nathaniel Isaacs's *Travels and Adventures in Eastern Africa*. We'll look at Isaacs again in Chapter 1, but for the moment consider the portrait of Shaka that appeared in that book, reproduced here. This purported to be 'taken from the life', after a drawing by Isaacs's companion in Zulu territory, James Saunders King. If it was, it

*The first portrayal of Shaka appeared in Nathaniel Isaacs's* Travels and Adventures in Eastern Africa *(1836). Purportedly drawn 'from the life' by James Saunders King, it is self-evidently inaccurate. Its kingly poise and conventionalised royal position on a rocky promontory completely contradict the portrait of degenerate brutality that Isaacs gives us in his text.*

became radically distorted in the process of etching and publication. Consider the stance: the head turned in profile, the hand curled round the spear, the weight taken on one leg and the other foot slightly raised. Now this is a well-used convention in European art called *contrapposto*; it goes back to antiquity, but can be found, for example, in Dürer's engraving of Adam, a Leonardo drawing of a soldier, through to any number of eighteenth-century depictions of 'Hottentot' and Xhosa chiefs. Combine this convention with the inaccurate skirt, assegai and shield, and we can be sure that what we have here is nothing like the real Shaka, but a mere collage of Eurocentric conventions and inventions.

This kind of thing has happened in the written portrayals, too. As a matter of fact, we have virtually no idea what Shaka looked like.

We need to go right back to the beginning. We need to pare away the fictions and reassess the evidence, such as it is, with a cool clear eye. What I present in this book is the fruits of a long process of reassessment, drawing on the work of several specialist scholars. This is, in some ways, a summary of my two more substantial books, *Savage Delight: White Myths of Shaka* (2000), and *Myth of Iron: Shaka in History* (2006). These are available for anyone interested in following up the minutiae of the historical arguments.

I'm often asked if I went out into the field and questioned Zulu elders. I did not, partly because I don't have the skills (others do, and are doing so, and will produce, probably, a very different biography of Shaka, which is as it should be). Partly, also, I reasoned thus: if a Zulu informant now has a story which has appeared earlier in the literature, I'll go with the earliest version; if there is no earlier appearance of that story, it is therefore by definition unverifiable. So what I have done is simply reassess all the earliest *written* sources we have to hand and see what emerges.

And what emerges is astonishingly different from the stereotype.

# 1

# Who do we trust?

*The problem of sources*

'Hear you are about to publish. Do make Chaka out to be as bloodthirsty as you can; it helps swell out the work and make it interesting.' This is from a historical document, words on a yellowing page. The history of Shaka is made up of a stew of such statements, some of which (like this one) tell us more about the writers than about Shaka.

Who is writing, to whom? When? Why would he make such a nasty request? What kind of 'work' does he have in mind, and to whom does he think it would be 'interesting'? What kind of people are the writer and his imagined reader? The historian needs to ask such questions of *any* historical document. The astonishing thing about the path that Shaka's story has taken over the last 170 years is that it has apparently remained immune to such investigation. Until very recently, few bothered or dared to ask the basic questions about the credibility of the sources. Few stopped and thought, now where did *that* story come from? Even professional historians recycled anecdotes which today seem absurd. Even worse, some historians actively *invented* stories, and one after another embellished them and repeated them, until outright speculation became 'the truth'.

Here's just one example. Henry Francis Fynn, one of the handful of white eyewitnesses of Shaka's reign, stated that Shaka had killed 'a million people'. You will still find this figure, and higher, repeated in today's literature. However, Fynn had no way of knowing any such thing: it was a thumb-suck based on a particular view of Shaka – Shaka as a kind of genocidal maniac, an unresting killing-machine. But *why* the inventive lie? It will not surprise you, perhaps, to discover that Fynn was the recipient of the plea we quoted at the start; he was the one 'about to publish'. The quotation is from a letter written in 1832 by another eyewitness to Shaka's reign, Nathaniel Isaacs. Was Fynn, then, simply heeding Isaacs's call to make Shaka out to be more 'bloodthirsty' than he was, because he knew his English readership would revel in stories of African savagery?

The answer is, partly. Fynn's claim was only made years after Shaka's death, in a letter to the Cape Governor: Fynn was bidding for a stretch of land which, allegedly, had been depopulated by Shaka. His right, he claimed, was based on a territorial grant from the Zulu king himself. Anyway (he insinuated), Shaka didn't deserve that land because he was such a brute, while he – Fynn – was a lonely, morally upright pioneer of civilisation. Fynn never got the land, because the colonial government knew well enough that Fynn was no such thing. In short, the claim of a million dead was uttered, or written, in a very specific context, for a very specific purpose – a purpose which had little or nothing to do with the historical reality of Shaka.

We need to go back to the beginning. Who *were* Isaacs, Fynn, James Saunders King, Francis Farewell, John Cane? What were they doing in Zulu country? They were eyewitnesses, to be sure, but sometimes eyewitnesses (even as we ultimately depend on them) are the *least* reliable sources. They are the ones with the most at stake. Why then did they write? How did their texts actually come into being?

Contemporary Cape government records, early newspapers, missionary accounts and Zulu traditions make it pretty clear. The adventurers were (as one early Zulu informant put it) 'people in poor or questionable circumstances at the Cape'. Farewell was a bluff, unemployed, ex-Navy man who had batted around the roughest trading ports of the world for some years – until he met James Saunders King, a wheedling sailor and wheeler-dealer who was likewise desperate for revenue. Together they persuaded Cape Town businessmen to rent them a boat for unspecified trade on Africa's east coast. En route, King had picked up a lost teenager – Nathaniel Isaacs – in St Helena. They sailed for Port Natal (Durban) in 1824, where Farewell, Fynn and a clutch of others were in the process of setting themselves up. Fynn was on the run, having robbed a store in the Eastern Cape hamlet of Bathurst. Unhappily, King wrecked his vessel on the sandbar across Port Natal's harbour mouth, temporarily cutting themselves off from 'civilisation'.

For five years, these men hunted for ivory, ran guns, fought as mercenaries both for and against the Zulu, set up their own private armies, probably offloaded the occasional slave and spawned a substantial number of children from local 'wives' (whom they subsequently abandoned). The Cape missionary Stephen Kay accused them of 'going native'.

None of this, predictably, surfaced in their own writings, which were in part attempted denials of Kay's revelations. The Cape government, too, viewed them with intense suspicion: it disowned the traders as far as it could without actually abandoning them. As the Cape Governor, Sir Lowry Cole, cautiously put it in 1828, Farewell and co. seemed 'in their intercourse with Chaka to have had no other object in view but their own personal advantage'. The humanitarian John Philip went further: 'Farewell and others have stirred up war wherever they have gone.'

King died in 1828, a month before Shaka did, Farewell shortly afterwards. Isaacs went on, doubtless having learned the skills of profitable violence during his time in Zulu country, to tour the slaving ports of the east coast. He tried to launch a bizarre scheme to get a Madagascar slave-lord to annex Natal. He ended up in West Africa, running illicit alcohol and then slaves from an island off Sierra Leone. The law eventually caught up with him, but the ship carrying all the evidence back to England – including the actual manacles from his slave island – went down in an Atlantic storm. Isaacs wriggled off. He died in bed in England in 1872.

Isaacs also died all but functionally illiterate; this much is clear from surviving correspondence. Yet just four years after he wrote that letter to Fynn, Isaacs produced a two-volume account of his time with Shaka, *Travels and Adventures in Eastern Africa* (1836). Although he had aired a few extracts in a Cape Town newspaper, the *South African Commercial Advertiser*, the book was the first major account of Shaka to reach the English-speaking public. In it, Isaacs did his level best to follow the advice he had given to Fynn. For Shaka, Isaacs wrote, 'the eve of going to war was always the period of brutal and inhuman murders, in which he seemed to indulge with as much savage delight as the tiger with his prey. When once he had determined on a sanguinary display of his power, nothing could restrain his ferocity; his eyes evinced his pleasure, his iron heart exulted, his whole frame seemed as if it felt a joyous impulse at seeing the blood of innocent creatures flowing at his feet; his hands grasped, his herculean and muscular limbs exhibiting by their motion a desire to aid in the execution of the victims of his vengeance ... a monster created with more than ordinary power and disposition for doing mischief, and from whom we recoil as we would at the serpent's hiss or the lion's growl.'

This kind of purple rhetoric is drawn from Gothic potboiler fictions, not from unvarnished observation. Unquestionably it was ghost-written by someone back in England, worked up to suit the expectations of an English audience – and it was their tastes that were bloodthirsty, not Shaka. Yet, despite its exaggerations, its gaps, its inner contradictions, its obvious agendas and cultural blindnesses, Isaacs's *Travels* has long been taken as essentially truthful. Isaacs is seen as the heroic youth, inexperienced and therefore unblemished, naïve but unaffected in his views. Though *Travels* purports to be based on actual diaries, we have no original documents to compare it with. It remains useful, but only if we read and judge it through the veils of alibi, cultural prejudice and rewriting.

We are luckier with Fynn. The archives hold

most of the original documents from which James Stuart compiled *The Diary of Henry Francis Fynn*, published only in 1950. We can see exactly what Stuart did – which was to cut and paste various fragments into continuous narrative, upgrade Fynn's appalling prose, fill in gaps, speculate, insert passages of his own and comprehensively obscure the originals, all in the service of valorising Fynn. Stuart footnoted that 'Fynn's discreet, courageous and humane bearing' had disarmed Shaka and 'even caused [Fynn] to be taken as typical of the race he belonged to'. Stuart's colonial agenda is clear, for at the time Fynn and co. had been regarded quite differently. The *Diary* is no diary; it is, as the historian Julian Cobbing has said, 'one of the major disasters of South African historiography'. It should be abandoned in favour of returning to Fynn's original papers, which are quite problematic enough in themselves – patchy, contradictory, self-regarding and often deliberately untruthful.

As for his subsequent colourful career as magistrate and agent amongst the Zulu and Xhosa peoples, Fynn was repeatedly arraigned for murdering chiefs in cold blood, beating Africans, rustling cattle and smuggling guns. His private horde of supporters in northern Mpondo country became known as the iziNkumbi – the Locusts – and he himself as 'Mbulazi', the Killer. He was just as nasty a piece of work as Isaacs.

Astoundingly, the history of Shaka has rested largely on the testimony of these two frontier ruffians, whose reputation was rapidly swung around to exactly the opposite of what it had been in the 1820s and 1830s. It suited the white settlers of the 1840s and after to spread this kind of propaganda. Natal's chief administrator in charge of Africans in the 1860s, Theophilus Shepstone (later largely responsible for engineering the 1879 war which finally shattered the Zulu state), used such propaganda in a manner calculated to discredit Shaka. Largely thanks to Shepstone, Fynn's exaggerations about the extent of Shaka's depredations and power became a crucial element in a wider imperial campaign: Shaka had killed off so many people that there were swathes of 'depopulated' land conveniently available for incoming colonists to occupy with nary a moral qualm. That this was untrue has now been proved beyond doubt. It was, effectively, the beginning of apartheid, and was a myth that would be used many decades later to justify it. It became, it's not too much to say, an unquestioned part of settler consciousness.

This consciousness permeates two other major works and their reception. The first is a tome unavoidable in Zulu studies, the priest-anthropologist A T Bryant's *Olden Times in Zululand and Natal* (1929). Floridly written and decidedly racist in its undertones, *Olden Times* has nevertheless seemed so dense with 'oral' stories and complexly interwoven detail about the peoples of the KwaZulu-Natal region that it has been treated as indispensable. However, careful scholarship, especially by the historian John Wright, has shown that what little is not based on Isaacs, Fynn and Shepstone is either uncorroborated or patently wrong. *Olden Times* can, surprisingly, be virtually dispensed with.

Bryant was the historical demi-god for many who followed, not least of all the famous E A Ritter, whose *Shaka Zulu* (1955) has appeared to be almost the solitary attempt by anyone to write a 'biography' of Shaka. It is nothing of the kind. The original manuscripts and correspondence in Durban's Don Africana Library make it perfectly clear that *Shaka Zulu* was written as a *novel* laden with inventions, soggy with the sentimental and wholly fictional love-story of Pampata, and spattered with gratuitous cruelty and gore. It was enriched, however, with a new heroism in the Shaka figure. This lionisation was seductive at the time – more politically correct – but in fact it is almost wholly invented. Moreover, Ritter was (as he said himself) a 'bush scientist', not a writer. He quoted reams from Bryant and wrote the rest badly. His London publisher, however, sensed a good story and turned the script over to a minor novelist named Edward Hyam. Hyam set about rewriting it, cut out about a third, and smoothed the style until it *sounded* more like a 'history'. And as such it was universally accepted. Many of the tales of Shaka with which we have become so familiar – the invention of the stabbing-spear, the dancing on devil-thorns, the slaughter of soldiers who got illicit erections, the 'battle of Qokli Hill' – derive from Ritter and nowhere else. They are fiction. *Shaka Zulu* possesses, in itself, no value whatsoever as a credible account.

So where can we go from here? Happily, apart from the archival sources already mentioned, we do have some counter-weights to the ponderous juggernaut of the popular picture. A lesser counterweight lies in other eyewitnesses. In their perpetual, petty squabbles with King and Fynn, Francis Farewell and John Cane revealed snippets of the reality through their few letters and interviews. More substantial is the testimony of Charles Rawden Maclean, who by some mysterious historical chemistry has come down to us as 'John Ross'. Maclean was even younger than Isaacs when wrecked at Port Natal – about twelve. He became a sort of pet to Shaka, spending more time with the Zulu king than the rest of the whites put together (their direct contact with Shaka was actually a matter of a few scattered months, at most). In the 1850s he began publishing an account of his experiences in the obscure *Nautical Magazine*. Though thinned by retrospect and evidently never completed, his account is markedly more measured than his compatriots'. He by no means whitewashes Shaka, but he adamantly denies the hysterical attributions of genocide and sadism and is warmly sympathetic towards the Zulu as a people. Unlike the slaver Isaacs, Maclean became a staunch opponent of the slave trade, operating from, and eventually dying on, the Caribbean island of St Lucia. He is, his youth at the time and cultural biases notwithstanding, an eminently more believable witness, and it's regrettable that his account is so slight.

So much for the white writers. There is a greater counter-weight. By one of the most extraordinary ironies of the whole story, the same James Stuart who fraudulently inflicted upon the world *The Diary of Henry Francis Fynn*, also worked astonishingly hard to collect the testimonies of dozens of the most knowledgeable African informants in the Zulu region. As an administrator and magistrate in Natal, Stuart, between about 1890 and 1920, filled notebook after notebook with carefully transcribed accounts of his conversations. Most of these have now been translated and published in the five volumes (so far) of *The James Stuart Archive*. It is the richest source we have of the view of history held by the Zulu themselves and (importantly) by some of their neighbours. This is the main source upon which the present book is based.

This material is as difficult to work with. It is not

intrinsically more truthful or accurate just because it is 'oral'. It, too, is contradictory, full of gaps, political biases, forgetfulness, propaganda, lies. It, too, was delivered by real people with real stakes in the situation of their own time and that of their fathers, many of whom had lived under Shaka's rule. By 1900 – seventy years after Shaka's death – all sorts of distortions and 'feedback loops' had insinuated themselves, rendering certain accounts quite unreliable. James Stuart's informants already lived in a profoundly different world. Mbovu kaMtshumayeli confessed, 'I no longer belong to the old generation. I am a seed that has dropped to a new state of civilisation. I take but little interest in former affairs.'

Often, we simply don't know enough about the informants to judge their credibility adequately. At least some informants we learn quite a lot about, and I'll have occasion to foreground them in the course of our narrative. Some of them were deeply knowledgeable about Zulu affairs and history, though they vilified or lionised Shaka, depending on where they were coming from. They were also aware of their own limitations: Mqaikana kaYenge lamented in 1916 that had he learned to really listen to the old folk and to write, 'I would have put down all my father told me, and read it nowadays. I allowed this to escape me.'

In short, there is practically no one we can trust

entirely. Often, we are just going to have to accept that there is much we will never know for sure. Most importantly of all, we need to remember that Shaka was not superhuman. He was a real person, living within real political, cultural and environmental constraints; this means certain explanations will be far more probable than others.

Taking all that into account, and reading all the available evidence for what it is, we at least have the basis for a new biography. Having interrogated every claim, pared away the obvious inventions, explored the motivations for the lies and corroborated accounts wherever possible, we can arrive at something closer to the elusive 'what happened'.

2

# He was not alone
*Shaka in context*

'There seems now no doubt that the aggressions of the Mantatees and all the other Tribes on each other is solely occasioned by the operation of that monster Chaca. He rules with despotic sway as far as Delagoa Bay down to Port Natal, and whenever he thinks proper to set off on one of his plundering and murderous excursions either North or South, he sets the whole of the Tribes in motion, he robs those nearest to him, murders, and burns their habitations … There appears no present remedy for it.'

That is the Eastern Cape settler Thomas Philipps, writing in 1827. By that time, sundry wild stories had filtered through from the adventurers at Port Natal – Fynn, King, Isaacs, Farewell – regarding the nefarious deeds of the Zulu despot. So many stories, in fact, that at least one newspaper correspondent commented sensibly: 'The frightful stories told of King Chaka, and which have for several years appeared in the English newspapers uncontradicted, are, we have reason to believe, mere fabrications. His enormous army, his shocking barbarities, and his projected conquests, partook too much of the marvellous … If Chaka cut down his subjects like hay, we suspect his army would dwindle to something less than thirty thousand men.'

Philipps's summary contains the seed of what would become known as the 'mfecane'. This was not a Zulu word, and only appeared in the 1920s as a kind of catch-all term for the explosion of violence associated with Shaka's rise to power and the founding of 'the Zulu nation'. Almost all the main elements of the 'mfecane' idea are contained in Philipps's paragraph: that the violence was 'solely' Shaka's doing, beginning and ending with him; that frightened 'tribes' scattered, carrying 'Zulu' methods of all-destructive warfare with them in a kind of domino effect; that Shaka ran his 'state' primarily through terror; and that through this terror Shaka seamlessly and singlehandedly controlled that whole vast region. In short, the 'mfecane' was the archetype, the model, for a self-destructive, self-contained vortex of black-on-black savagery. It was a model of obvious usefulness for both the architects of imperial rule and, later, apartheid apparatchiks.

With superficial variations, the 'mfecane' model persists to the present. In John Omer-Cooper's well-known book, *The Mfecane Aftermath* (1966), it was given something of a positive 'nation-building' gloss, as if Shaka were somehow heroically ushering the Zulu into a modern, nationalistic age. But the language of violence remained: Shaka was a 'volcano', 'the eye of the storm', 'voracious', a 'flood', and so on – as if he were some sort of inexplicable, unstoppable natural force – a 'ball, not of snow', as the settler Cowper Rose rightly scoffed in 1828.

Such early voices of scepticism were comprehensively buried. We now know, however, that the 'mfecane' model is simply untenable. In a way, this whole book will be devoted to overturning it, but we can outline three main reasons in this chapter. Firstly, the Zulu were never completely isolated from the outside world. Although the region between Delagoa Bay and Port Natal (Maputo and Durban) was less frequented by foreigners than regions further north and further south, it was not ignored. True, the coastline was short on harbours and navigable rivers. 'The beach was very foul and full of steep rocks', one traveller grumbled. So mariners tended not to land here, unless shipwrecked by the frequent storms. Numbers of parties of stranded Europeans slogged their way up or down the coastline; many were speared or starved. But a startling number stayed to add their genes to the local pool.

More importantly, to the north and east, the African coast had been the target of traders and slavers for centuries. It was not so far to Mozambique, one of the most horrific of slaving ports from the seventeenth century onwards. Just across the waters, Madagascar was a prime slaving way-station. While Delagoa Bay was less attractive to raiders and entrepreneurs, slaves and ivory, iron, food and hides still flowed out, while beads, cloth, copper and brass flowed in. Indeed, beads had been an integral part of south-east African societies for decades before Shaka's time and were probably the main currency for *lobolo* – bride-price or dowry – until cattle replaced them in the nineteenth century.

Around 1750, the volume of trade in both goods and slaves boomed. In the 1770s, at least 75 000 pounds of ivory left Delagoa Bay annually. Trade climbed steadily until the early 1800s, then there seemed to be a bit of a lull. In the 1820s, by which time Shaka was well established in power, it exploded again. Actual numbers are impossible to come by; too much was illegal and was never recorded. However, we know that after 1811, when Brazilian markets opened up, 10 000 slaves a year were being exported from Mozambique; a decade later it was up to 20 000. Between 1825 and 1830 Rio de Janeiro alone imported 4000 slaves from Delagoa Bay. These are just the official figures. When you consider that, in general, an estimated five people died for every slave exported, the impact looks quite devastating.

Control of the pestilential settlement at Delagoa Bay shifted between Portuguese and Austrian companies. Renegade Englishmen ran river boats manned by Goanese Indians. Local economies served American whalers. Madagascan pirates in ocean-going canoes plundered everyone. Generally these multinational foreigners relied on local traders to deliver the goods. Trade routes reached well into Zulu territory; some even spanned the sub-continent.

Where they could, both European and African groups fomented local conflicts in order to generate slaves. When a British naval surveyor, W F W Owen, visited Delagoa Bay in 1822–3, he found hundreds of slaves ready for shipment and evidence of continuous 'traffick with the natives for Ivory, Rhinoceros horns, tiger Skins, Cattle, Slaves and Hoes'. He thought the trade in humans sufficient 'to keep the neighbouring tribes in a ferment and a continual state of warfare'. This is the unholy duo that characterises slavery everywhere: a spiral of mutually reinforcing warfare and enslavement.

At the same time, to the south and west, another European encroachment had been steadily gaining ground since 1652. The tiny Dutch garden and way-station established at the Cape by Jan van Riebeeck expanded in fits and starts into a runaway colonial occupation under the British. While appalling violence was developing in southern Mozambique, equally vicious conflicts were occurring between white settlers and Khoi, San and Xhosa indigenous peoples right up to the Great Fish River. By Shaka's time, these dynamics of violence were well established. Moreover, by the early 1800s, mounted bands of Griqua and Koranna marauders were raiding violently into an arc across the Caledon and Orange River valleys, just north of the Thukela–Phongolo river catchment.

We can envisage the catchment – now mostly KwaZulu-Natal – being caught in the jaws of an enormous pincer. How hard the pincer bit from year to year, decade to decade, depended on all sorts of outside factors: weather, ocean currents, wars between European nations, changes in international law, opening up or closing down of distant markets, currency fluctuations. Almost plumb in the middle of this scene, the Zulu clanlet would find itself partly buffered by surrounding peoples, but not unaffected, either. In short, the geographic isolationism of the mainstream 'mfecane' model doesn't hold.

Secondly, the 'mfecane' cannot be isolated in time. Major changes were happening over a longer period than just in the 1810s. It has often been assumed that precolonial societies in the southern African region were uniformly village-based, run by family heads and consisting of small, independent, closely related units. Sons would conventionally marry outside the family and eventually split off to form new settlements or *imizi*, with independent genealogies. This is often misleadingly portrayed as a kind of peaceful idyll. However, what slender evidence we have about pre-Shakan times suggests that there were sometimes also looser, fluctuating and conflictual allegiances of wider kinds. Archaeology and oral traditions show that violence had been on the increase at least since 1750, thirty years before Shaka was born. Shaka did not erupt into a timeless idyll like some inexplicable cataclysm. Moreover, violence continued, for many reasons, well after Shaka had died, culminating with total white colonisation in the late nineteenth century. Shaka was part of a continuum.

So a third reason why the 'mfecane' model doesn't hold is that political developments in response to the violence were *not* centred on Shaka's Zulu. Around 1750, it is now clear, slaving, trade, violence, the use of defensive hilltop settlement, and more centralised and militarised groupings were developing, all at much the same time, right across the region. By 1800 or so, the little Zulu were already surrounded by a ring of 'states' or polities which were centralising and militarising in a variety of ways. Shaka would learn from *them*, not the other way round. Violence and other societal changes took a number of different forms, over a spray of different centres and vectors, of which the Zulu eventually became only one, albeit the most successful. All in all, the concept of the 'mfecane' as some sort of distinct and self-contained 'movement' or 'phase' makes no geographical, chronological or political sense of things.

Nevertheless, a quite profound social change was happening, throughout the Thukela–Phongolo catchment and over the course of the three-quarters of a century from the 1750s onwards. Why?

In 1988 the historian Julian Cobbing published an article in which he argued that the slave trade, and not Shaka, was the main motor of violence and political centralisation in the region in the first two decades of the nineteenth century. He was greeted with howls of protest. Because there was no firm evidence of *how many* slaves were exiting Delagoa Bay in the 'crucial period' (the 1810s), nor of exactly how slaving might have impacted on inland societies, Cobbing was said to have failed to make the case. But Cobbing both forced historians to look closely at the evidence again and, perhaps more importantly, embedded the Zulu irretrievably in the broader, subcontinental picture. His basic insights hold: slaving *was* happening; it had *some* impact on many groups; and it happened alongside extensive trade of other kinds.

In opposition, some historians have proposed that

over-population with its ecological consequences was the key. Some argue that the advent of maize provided for a population explosion. Maize, however, only became a staple diet in the nineteenth century. Others have blamed drought. In this theory, drought stimulates more aggressive competition for resources, and so more people band defensively together. There is no firm evidence that such timely droughts occurred, and they were anyway more likely to make people scatter, not congregate. Still other historians have argued, more plausibly, that international trade provoked greater competition. This is probably true up to a point – except that trade in almost anything bar weaponry depends on peace, not warfare. It's more likely that something else, something new, was stimulating centralisation, and that sometimes centralised militarism *then* enabled some people to attack trade caravans, raid more successfully for cattle or bully other groups into paying tribute. Such conflict was likely a result, not a cause.

One last thing needs explaining: the most tightly and successfully militarised groups developed first near Delagoa Bay, and then moved almost without exception southwards or westwards *away* from the Bay. Nearest the Bay, the Tsonga-Thembe group partly militarised; they never became very formidable, but traded brass and copper far inland and sometimes raided on their own account. Hence the Mabhudu moved a short way south of the Bay and became a very sturdy polity, which long outlasted Shaka's. They were in turn partly responsible for pushing the Dlamini-Swazi Tlokwa and Ngwane groups west across the Lubombo hills and on to the highveld.

The Ndwandwe, Jere and Gaza – inter-related, future slaver-states – also moved or were pushed west. As recent work by John Wright shows, the Ndwandwe would become easily the most aggressive of all the groups, certainly surpassing the Zulu. They were settled by 1800 just south of the Phongolo River and were raiding west and south with unusual ferocity long before Shaka rose to prominence. We know very little about the Ndwandwe, but the only really persuasive explanation for that ferocity is that they were raiding not for the usual cattle, but for people. In response, the Ngwane and Hlubi groups toughened their organisational structures as well as shifting westwards to around the headwaters of the Mzinyathi River.

Further south, on the lower Mhlathuze River, the Mthethwa under Jobe, and then his son Dingiswayo, did likewise. The Mthethwa would become the main resistance to the Ndwandwe – and it was to the Mthethwa that the smaller Zulu clan were paying tribute when Shaka was born. South of them again, across the Thukela River, the Chunu and the Thembu, the Mkhize and the Qwabe, were also centralising to varying degrees.

Most of these groups were developing forms of semi-militarised age-groupings of men – *amabutho* – led by more specialised leaders, or *izinduna*. All of them were concentrating more control over rituals such as the first-fruits (*umkhosi*) ceremonies, over rain-making, over the distribution of women, in the hands of single over-arching leaders. All of them were using these structures, at first to present sturdier defences against outside aggressors; later, perhaps almost by accident, they committed aggressions on their own account. Interestingly, circumcision was also on the wane; at least in the case of the Mthethwa and the Zulu, this was explicitly tied to increased demands on young men to be ready and fit for fighting duty. Alongside this, women were being gathered into a tighter structure, what would become a central feature of several groups including the Zulu: the *isigodlo*. The *isigodlo* was both an architectural palisade at the heart of the settlement, tightly and defensively controlled, and the collection of women included within that space. These women were increasingly the prerogative of the overlord, the *inkosi*, to dispense in marriage.

So, profound social changes were growing out of the existing structures and rituals, freshly laden with a sense of regional threat. Though the case is not closed, it seems to me that slaving, abetted by other competitive trade, is the best candidate to explain this. As the doyen of African historians, Basil Davidson, has written of similar scenarios elsewhere on the continent: 'the slave trade became inseparable from the workings of … strong chiefs and kings … Wherever it failed to find them, it caused them to come into being.'

The Zulu, for the moment, found themselves sheltered by their allegiance to the more powerful Mthethwa, but as early as the 1780s they were feeling the pressures of aggressors from the north. Into this situation, Shaka was born.

3

# Beetle or axe?
*Ancestry, birth and childhood*

'A man of the Langeni went out one day from eNguga, accompanied by a youth, his baggage carried by a smaller boy. Out in the veld they found Senzangakhona and other boys, herding cattle. They slaughtered young steers, ones with horns broader than the width of a hand. Senzangakhona gave them meat; they ate; they went on with their errands. On their return, Senzangakhona fed them again. When they got home to Langeni country, they related the story to the girls, including Nandi. "Who was this man who gave you meat?" Nandi asked. "It was Senzangakhona," they said. "How I wish to see him!" Nandi exclaimed. The man replied, "I could show him to you."'

So begins a romantic version of Shaka's beginnings, as told by Ndlovu kaThimuni, one of James Stuart's informants. Ndlovu goes on to relate, in great detail, how Nandi falls accidentally pregnant. The elders of her Langeni people try to cover it up by claiming she has an *itshati*, a 'troublesome intestinal beetle'. For a time the baby is hidden from the Zulu chief-in-waiting, Senzangakhona. A Zulu man named Mudli is at the centre, hiding the child with Senzangakhona's mother. The truth will out, of course; Senzangakhona hears of it; he wants to kill the child; Mudli smuggles him away to safety. Shaka – so named after the beetle – spends the rest of his childhood in exile. Nandi and Senzangakhona never do marry.

This is the story related by A T Bryant, then by Ritter, and thenceforward by everyone else. The great warrior-hero was named after a *beetle*? It's funny, ironic and irresistible. But is it true? *Shaka*, after all, could also mean a bowel complaint (Fynn thought it meant 'dysentery') or merely 'early pregnancy'. It could also mean, as we shall see later, 'axe'.

Ndlovu kaThimuni has a particular position in relation to this story. When he met James Stuart in 1902, he was 45, 'talkative, agreeable, intelligent'. His main source was his own father Thimuni, who had been called up into Shaka's army in about 1826. Thimuni had come of age, though, in Dingane's reign, so the stories he passed on were often malicious tales concocted by Dingane to discredit his predecessor. For this and other reasons, Ndlovu is likely to be a vector for anti-Shaka stories. But his story was not the only one in circulation. Even his own brother Mruyi disagreed with him. Stuart himself picked the holes in Ndlovu's version. How could Shaka have formally been so named, if it were not by his own father? And how did *itshati* get distorted into 'Shaka' anyway; wasn't the beetle actually called *ikamba*? Why was all protocol avoided and the birth reported to Mudli, instead of to the *inkosi* of the time, Jama? Most importantly, wasn't it the *minority* opinion at the time?

Ndlovu had no convincing answers to these questions. But before we outline the *majority* opinion about Shaka's birth, let's go back a bit in time. What of Shaka's ancestry?

We don't know where the Zulu 'came from'. Some thought they immigrated from somewhere on higher ground – 'rolled down in a grain-basket', as the idiom colourfully had it. But it seems more likely, on the whole, that they developed as self-conscious Zulu pretty much where they remained for the rest of their history: along the White Mfolozi between Nhlazatshe and present-day Mgungundlovu. Shaka's ancestors lived here and were buried here.

Those earlier ancestors are shrouded in obscurity and legend. Jama is the first known Zulu chieftain, or *inkosi*, to have people *khonza* to him – to swear allegiance or pay tribute. Among them were the Mabaso and the Buthelezi, families who would be so closely integrated with 'the Zulu', right up to the present, that it becomes almost impossible to say where the boundaries are. In fact, genetically speaking, there *are* no boundaries. The principles of exogamy ensured that, as the political entity expanded and absorbed women and men from neighbouring groups, whatever might be called 'Zulu' inevitably and mathematically became progressively thinned. So to say that there remains some kind of 'pure Zulu' core is extremely dubious. And to say, as so many white writers have, that there is some uniquely aggressive 'blood strain' in 'the Zulu' is rubbish.

Jama died when his heir designate, Senzangakhona, was still a youth. We have no idea how long he had reigned, but he probably flourished between the 1750s and 1770s. He passed on a family network which itself paid tribute to the much larger Mthethwa polity. The Mthethwa were probably already in a state of growth under Jobe, father of the more famous Dingiswayo. Senzangakhona and Dingiswayo were probably more or less contemporaries, assuming their respective mantles at about the same time: 1780.

Under both Jama and Senzangakhona, Zulu influence expanded parasitically, as it were, within the belly of the larger Mthethwa state. Jama was able to pass on an *ibutho* or three to his young heir. (The term *ibutho* is ill served by the translation 'regiment': only some duties of this age- or place-based grouping would be 'military'. They were just as much, even under Shaka, 'multi-purpose labour gangs', in Bryant's phrase.) Probably there was a period of regency before Senzangakhona could formally take up the chieftaincy. (We should also avoid talk of 'kings' and 'thrones'; these were as yet very small patrimonies.) And it was probably during this regency – headed perhaps by Shaka's great-aunt Mnkabayi – that a certain unexpected child was born.

What of Shaka's parents? We know little about Nandi, a name meaning 'sweet one'. Her father was chieftain of the nearby Langeni clan, a link of enduring importance to the Zulu. It suited the white adventurers to depict Nandi as a vicious fishwife of 'violent disposition', but there is no real evidence to support this. She's remembered fondly in Zulu lore.

We know more about Senzangakhona. He was, most accounts agree, rather colourless, having few idiosyncrasies or *imikhuba*. Senzangakhona is also depicted in his praises, his *izibongo*, as a bit of a dresser, a ladies' man, a somewhat frivolous hunter, with an unpredictable streak: 'Gurgling water of the Mpembeni stream, I don't even know where it's going to, some runs downhill and some runs uphill.' Still, he was seen as doing his best to secure the interests of his people. Nathaniel Isaacs claimed Senzangakhona 'kept the neighbouring tribes around him in great terror and subjection', but the *izibongo* picture more of a negotiator: 'He who went with criticism and returned with praises ... who spoke and his words were resisted but presently accepted.' Most think he did not have a huge following and even had a hard time succeeding to the position of *inkosi*, having to kill his brother Mkhasana to get it. Shaka was born into the middle of this imbroglio.

So here's the big question: was Shaka illegitimate or not? This question came to reflect on whether Shaka should have been the Zulu leader or not. People who, then or later, supported his candidacy would be likely to say he was legitimate; his opponents, naturally, that he wasn't. How, then, did both kinds of story arise in the first place?

As we've mentioned, the idea of Shaka's illegitimacy was the minority opinion. Even the white eyewitnesses, who might be expected to seize upon such a juicy morsel, never alleged it. As far as the contemporary evidence shows, Shaka was born legitimately, and Senzangakhona *did* marry Nandi. The illegitimacy story was pure slander.

Yet the circumstances of the birth were just uncertain enough for the illegitimacy line to take a firm hold – though it did so only after Shaka was dead. The consensus of the matter seems to be this: Nandi was an *isingodosi*, a maiden betrothed to Senzangakhona. While the couple awaited Senzangakhona's arrival at full maturity, they were permitted to *soma*, or *hlobonga* – to have non-penetrative sexual play. The passionate accident occurred.

This could hardly have been unusual or unknown. The problem was that Senzangakhona had not yet been circumcised; he had not been properly initiated into manhood. The pregnancy violated a whole raft of taboos and ritual procedures. Senzangakhona had to be hurriedly circumcised; then the *lobolo* was paid, and the marriage proceeded as normal. Shaka was born – just – within the bounds of propriety.

Nandi became only one of a large number of Senzangakhona's wives, many with sons. This would prove to be a complication for the succession, but not for another thirty years. That's how long Senzangakhona ruled. (This is to extend the timeframe a little further than most have allowed: generally, I think the evidence favours a longer, slower view of all the region's developments, instead of the Shaka-centred, explosive one.) Most people have based their estimate of Shaka's birthdate on a single opinion: that of the white adventurer James Saunders King. King, meeting Shaka in 1824, figured he was about 38, thus placing his birthdate in 1786. For no obvious reason, the date of 1787 is usually cited. If, however, we correlate a number of other events with the ages of various Zulu informants and note that Shaka was already going grey-haired and arthritic in 1824, there's a fairly strong argument for pushing it back to at least 1781. That is, however, little more than an informed guess.

So what happened to Shaka in the first thirty years of his life? As in the case of Jesus, we have some information about his birth, riddled with legend; a great deal more about the last years of his life; and not a great deal about the period in between. Rather like Jesus, such accounts as we have were contradictorily written up decades later. And like Jesus, Shaka is assumed by most to have gone into exile somewhere. This is the next phase of the romantic line, as related by Ndlovu kaThimuni.

The story became popular that either soon after his birth, or when he was a small boy, Nandi and Shaka were chased away by an angry Senzangakhona. Our informants are hopelessly divided about the cause and course of this alleged exile. The most common story is that he spent most of it as a persecuted outsider amongst the Langeni, his mother's people. The majority of informants, however, dismiss all this as pure fabrication. Only one contemporary source, Charles Rawden Maclean, claimed that Shaka had left home 'as an infant' – some indication that the story *might* have arisen during Shaka's lifetime. Shaka might have put it about himself. The 'exile' story seems, in some ways, to have been a kind of metaphor, a symbolic parable of rejection-and-return, used by more than one leader-hero in history to justify or dramatise an otherwise dodgy accession.

As it happens, there are several bits of more mundane information – the kind that is less subject to romanticisation – to show that Shaka almost certainly spent a more or less ordinary boyhood, right there in the Zulu heartland. Where traditions surface about the vital ritual phases of Shaka's life – the naming ceremony, his first nocturnal emission, and the piercing of his ears (*qumbuza*) – they are remembered as having happened in Zulu country. Interestingly, he was probably named Sikiti for his first twenty-odd years.

Shaka-Sikiti probably did spend time amongst the Langeni, his mother's people. This would have been perfectly natural, but it might also have given the 'exile' idea a certain traction. While he was there – so it was said – he was severely bullied. He had hot curds poured on his hands; boys trapped him with faeces buried in holes; he had to drink downstream of others. These anecdotes are either very ordinary or fiction; they do nothing to explain Shaka's psyche. In fact, they boil down really to one persistent idea: that he was in conflict with his Langeni cousin Makhedama. The usual story is that they had a squabble over some stones, representing cattle or bulls, in a game they were playing. This anecdote is, however, usually told in relation to much *later* conflict between these two robust leaders. The first phase of the conflict seems to have been in relation to a Langeni succession dispute, in which Sikiti somehow became involved. As we'll see, the rivalry simmered on for many years. The 'stone bulls' story is almost certainly a colourful metaphor for one or other of these later confrontations.

At the same time as Makhedama was wrestling for ascendancy over the Langeni, Sikiti was running foul of Zulu internal politics. He had been inducted in his late teens into his father's iWombe *ibutho*, or semi-military age-formation. This is another strong indication that Sikiti had never gone into exile at all. The iWombe remained one of his favourite units: it was *his* outfit. Very likely he began forging liaisons here with key allies who would be useful to him later. Almost certainly, in short, Nathaniel Isaacs was as close to the truth as we're likely to get: 'As Chaka *advanced towards manhood* [he] attracted the notice and ultimately the jealousy of his father, who resolved that he should die … Chaka's precocity, shrewdness and cunning soon enabled him to learn the intention of his father; and he fled … to a neighbouring tribe, called the Umtatwas.' Although the details of this defection remain fuzzy, Shaka-Sikiti did go to the Mthethwa. It is one of the few undisputed facts of Shaka's life.

4

# Learning the craft
*Shaka comes to power, c. 1800–1812*

'The Mthethwa would go into people's huts and seize the gourds and pour the contents into their mouths, to such an extent did they believe themselves masters of the land they passed through.' This was, at least for some, the prevailing image of Mthethwa methods. In contrast, A T Bryant pictured Dingiswayo as the 'Knight Chivalrous', mostly as a counterpoint to the allegedly Satanic tyrant Shaka. I suggest it was all a little more complex than either depiction.

Dingiswayo took over from his father Jobe in about 1780. Over a decade or more, he set about building up a polity (it was more than a chiefdom but not quite a state) sturdy enough to withstand increasing raiding pressure from the Ndwandwe. He established a number of *amabutho*, led by *izinduna*. He had an *isigodlo* of considerable size. From this basis he could establish marriage links with a growing number of neighbouring groups, conquering and assimilating some of them, and forging alliances with others. Sometimes Dingiswayo's conquest involved a targeted assassination; in the historian Carolyn Hamilton's words, 'It was Dingiswayo's policy to remove recalcitrant chiefs and to replace them with minors or known Mthethwa loyalists from amidst their ranks.' On the whole, Dingiswayo's overlordship was administered fairly lightly. People would come 'under his armpit' not only because they were bullied into doing so, but because they recognised the benefits: a local chief might lose some control over his men, his women and his ritual functions, but in return he could be better protected from outside threats.

By the time it reached its peak, the Mthethwa polity reached roughly from the Mhlathuze River in the south, to across the lower Mfolozi River in the north, and maybe up to a hundred kilometres inland: a blunt triangle between today's Richard's Bay, St Lucia and, inland, Vryheid. Its boundaries would have been fluid, its levels of control patchy, but it was the foundation upon which Shaka could eventually build. Much of what Dingiswayo practised, Shaka would adopt and adapt in later years. This wasn't confined to military tactics; there were much subtler social and political strategies to be learned as well.

At least some of Dingiswayo's ability to command seems to have derived from trade links with the outside world. The evidence is slight (based almost entirely on a couple of doubtful paragraphs from Fynn). However, the ancestral Mthethwa name, Nyambose, was well known at Delagoa Bay; it was a link on which Shaka certainly tried to capitalise later.

In 1800 or so, Sikiti-Shaka was already learning about the seamy side of politics. As we mentioned in the last chapter, he had probably got embroiled in the initial stages of a Zulu succession dispute, with Senzangakhona trying to whip some of his unruly sons into line. The dispute exploded when Sigujana, senior wife Bhibhi's son but one of the younger boys, was pronounced the chosen successor. This was not supported by a number of the influential women. The situation was only made worse by Senzangakhona's announcement that the men of the iWombe were not to be permitted to marry. (Shaka was not the first to do this; it was undoubtedly meant to keep more fighting men available in trying times.) A predictable result was that many of the men went off looking for sexual satisfaction anyway. Their *hlobonga*-ing with unauthorised women gave Senzangakhona the pretext for sending his sons away. Only Sigujana remained.

Sikiti went back to the Langeni. There, he ran into conflict with his cousin Makhedama, who himself was wresting control of the clan after the death of his father, Mgabhi. Makhedama was, by all accounts, both ferocious and self-centred. He became a vigorous, even vicious leader. He used, it is said, a short-hafted stabbing-spear – the one which Shaka is mistakenly credited with 'inventing' – saying grimly, 'Are people like buck that they should be stabbed at a distance?' Even more alarmingly, he is said to have impaled people with assegais, laying them on their backs and driving barbed assegais in through the neck, breastbone, or hands.

Perhaps because of this very ferocity, several Langeni men decided to hive off and *khonza* Dingiswayo directly. Sikiti went with them, turning up at the *umuzi* of one of Dingiswayo's elder statesmen, Ngomane kaMqomboli. If I'm correct about Sikiti's birthdate (c. 1781) and correct that he defected to the Mthethwa in his early manhood, he probably arrived on Ngomane's doorstep in about 1803. He would spend nearly a decade under Dingiswayo's wing. It's a decade we know next to nothing about.

Later romanticists would claim that Dingiswayo wouldn't have won a battle without Sikiti. This is certainly nonsense. Sikiti was presumably inducted into one of Dingiswayo's *amabutho*. He may even have become an *induna*, as he began to distinguish himself in battle. But we possess few details of such battles. Some tell of Sikiti's reckless courage in Dingiswayo's campaigns and hint at the beginnings of his involvement in regional politics. He is said in several anecdotes to have exceeded his brief, even as a noted warrior, an *iqawe*. Sent out by Dingiswayo to attack Malusi of the Nxumalo people, he launched himself alone into battle, stabbing ferociously about. Dingiswayo reproved him, telling him the son of a chief shouldn't be courting danger like that.

Sikiti certainly learned much of the arts of fighting under Dingiswayo, not to mention the cunning arts of statesmanship. He acquired some praises: 'Heavens that thunder in the open, where there is neither thorn nor mimosa tree; willow tree which overhangs the deep pool.' Dingiswayo himself sang of him, 'He whose fame spreads even while he is sitting.'

And it was Dingiswayo who gave Shaka, the man up to then called Sikiti, his more famous name, praising: 'Shaka who is not beaten, the axe that surpasses other axes, the impetuous one who disregards warnings.'

There are anecdotes of unlikely, boyish heroism, but also of defeats – as well as stories of a less savoury kind. Shaka had the habit, it was said, of ambushing commoners' girls on the bush paths; he would have intercourse and impregnate them. Dingiswayo would just shrug and say, 'What can one do with this wrongdoer from the Zulu (*itshinga la kwa Zulu*)?' The informants hesitate to say 'rape'. It's difficult to know how much weight to give such stories. They may well be coloured by malicious hindsight. Interestingly, more than one source claims Shaka had a wife or wives among the Mthethwa and at least one son, Zibizendhlela. If so, they were subsequently disowned, or 'given away' in an acceptable traditional style.

The traditional memory-bank – and the popular literature, too – is, however, dominated by one story from this period. It's a moment of irresistible, Oedipal interest. Here is one of the many variations, told by the brother to Ndlovu kaThimuni whom we've already met. Mruyi kaThimuni related:. 'Senzangakhona was sent for by Dingiswayo. He went to Dingiswayo in company with my grandfather Mudli and *amakosikazi* [great wives]. A hut was set apart for him. In one hut, whilst seated there with Dingiswayo, a large number of young men of Dingiswayo's tribe entered the hut by pre-arrangement. Shaka also came in, unknown at that time to Senzangakhona. He stood as if there were no place for him; he did this on instructions from the Mtetwa chief, i.e. according to a preconcerted plan. Shaka had on horns about his neck and the *iziqu* amulets of a man who had killed in battle; he was, moreover, one of Dingiswayo's heroes. He stood for a moment and looked about for a place to sit down, and before finding one, stood immediately before Senzangakhona so that his shadow fell on his father, and as soon as he had done this he sat down. A silence fell upon all in the hut. Dingiswayo asked Senzangakhona, "Do you see your calf here?" Senzangakhona was silent, and looked about among the young men. He then pointed at Shaka. Dingiswayo laughed, and proceeded to sing Shaka's praises. Senzangakhona's wives then one and all moved forward and kissed Shaka's arm. Shaka then asked Senzangakhona for an assegai. A number of assegais were produced and he was presented with one of them. Again was the young hero praised by the Mtetwa people, after which ordinary conversation took place for some time.'

That night – most versions have it – Senzangakhona went to sleep in the hut he'd been given. Some time during the night, he was awakened by water dripping through the thatch; a figure was seen slipping away into the darkness. Everyone 'knew' it was Shaka, washing himself with medicines over his father's head, effectively condemning him – just as the shadow would have done – to his death. True enough, Senzangakhona sickened, was taken away and died. The path was clear.

Whatever the truth of this (and there are sundry variations), the symbolism is obvious. The shadow; the magic of medicines; Senzangakhona selecting and handing over an assegai – all are symbolic of the transfer of power. Another version makes this even clearer. In this one, Senzangakhona hands Shaka an assegai; Shaka dances with it; then steps over to his brother

Sigujana – the designated heir – seated observing to one side, and taps him on the head with the blade. Sure enough, not many weeks later, when Sigujana is out fighting a neighbouring clan, he is struck fatally on the head, exactly where Shaka had touched him. Now, most are agreed that Sigujana was actually killed when Shaka took over power. This anecdote is purely symbolic, a legend meant to illuminate the later reality, not tell us exactly what happened.

The traditions are deeply divided about Shaka's coup, if that's what it was. There is no agreement even about when Senzangakhona died. Some said he died on the way home, either from Shaka's medicines or from sheer fright; others that he died some considerable time later; yet others that he was still alive when Shaka arrived with a massive column of Mthethwa in support. The trader and hunter David Leslie heard in 1865 that Senzangakhona died perfectly peacefully in his bed.

In one account, a whole deathbed speech is given to Senzangakhona. It's probably apocryphal, but it captures a sense of deep ambivalence about Shaka's succession. 'People of Zulu, I am dying. You must abandon the idea of appointing as chief my son [Sigujana]. For when I die there will come up the madman who was borne by a woman of Mbengi's people [Nandi]. He, Shaka, is not human. If you argue that he is not a chief he will kill my people, and destroy them. You must make him chief. For he will not be made chief by me; he will make himself chief.' Or, in another version, he says, 'Let this matter that we were talking about [viz. appointing Sigujana as heir] not be discussed; let it be avoided, because Shaka is among the Mthethwa *where we are ruled*.'

That Shaka *did* have Mthethwa support is undisputed. He arrived not only with a band of Mthethwa warriors, who stayed until the dust had settled, but also with a circle of prominent men who would stand by him for the rest of his reign. These included not only some Mthethwa, but Thembu, Qwabe and Langeni people. Right from the beginning, Shaka's closest circle would be something of a hotchpotch. He also brought a large number of Mthethwa cattle with which he could start his patronage of the necessary leading people. He strode, it was said, into the cattle enclosure of Nobamba, crying, 'Where are the cattle for my father's funeral?' And he began to slaughter those he had brought, 'slaughtered them as if he were destroying the herd'.

Irresistible Mthethwa support is one reason why Shaka took over relatively unopposed. Another is that there seemed to be a strong faction within the Zulu which backed him, including the apparently indomitable 'kingmaker', his great aunt Mnkabayi.

And a third reason is that such opposition as existed was swiftly dispatched. Sigujana was killed (though there is no evidence that Shaka himself did the dirty deed). So was Mudli, the man supposed to have rescued Shaka as a child. If *that* story was true, this murder seems unlikely. More plausibly, there are hints of complex negotiations between Dingiswayo and Mudli, in which Mudli declines to support Shaka's claim to the chieftaincy; Dingiswayo decreed that he had to be done away with.

But no more than a handful died. Compared to Dingane's take-over in 1828, Shaka's accession was relatively bloodless and relatively calmly accepted. Indeed, among most Zulu, Shaka would, in positive contrast to his brother-successor, be remembered as the one who 'killed none of his relations' – or almost none. Because traditional leadership was still, even among the more centralised polities, heavily dependent on family and close kinship structures, without internal family support Shaka would have got nowhere.

Perhaps, in the main, the Zulu saw that Shaka was their best hope at a time when the country appeared to be under greater threat of external violence than ever before. The period up to 1810 or 1812, when Shaka took over, had been something of a breathing space in the Thukela–Phongolo catchment. The next decade would prove dramatically different.

5

# The bulls of the herd
*Shaka and the north, 1812–1824*

'Shortly after Shaka's accession, Zwide attacked Dingiswayo; then disturbances broke out in every direction. Men were sent one way, only to be sent another after returning from a bloody and successful mission. Presently the whole country was upside-down, and it continued until subdued by Shaka's energetic action.' This is Ndlovu kaThimuni's summary of several years of Zulu history – accurate as far as it goes. We'll need to give it a little nuance.

One thing must be stressed before we go on: although we'll deal only with activities north of the Mhlathuze River in this chapter, they were never fully separate from the politics of the south, which are covered in Chapter 6. Nor were they separate from the internal matters of the polity, which we'll outline in Chapter 7. It's a mistake to separate too rigidly 'military' actions from 'civil' developments, or 'foreign' from 'domestic': they were inextricable and interdependent. But this way we can extract some clearer narrative threads.

As Ndlovu testifies, Shaka was *not* the motor of violence in the Thukela–Phongolo catchment. As a young warrior he had begun to participate in it, but only by way of conducting minor raids on nearby peoples at Dingiswayo's behest. As a novice chieftain he continued in much the same vein. I calculate that Shaka was boosted into the Zulu chieftaincy around the time that Napoleon Bonaparte invaded Russia: 1812. He continued to function as a sub-chief within the Mthethwa polity for another few years, with only partial independence. At the same time, he began to build up a sturdier polity of his own. Together – with Shaka as a *very* junior partner – they were essentially building up a defensive redoubt against the Ndwandwe.

First, then, Dingiswayo tried to strengthen the allegiances of those little groups lying between the Mthethwa and the Ndwandwe. There's an important point here: strategies varied with different groups, who responded with varying degrees of willingness and resistance. Some, like the Ntshalini, even Shaka never got the better of. The emerging bigger 'states' were all patchworks, fluid with intricate politicking and *ad hoc* decisions.

The groups in this 'buffer zone' were not the only people attacked. The Ndwandwe were conducting raids on a previously unknown scale right across their northern and western marches, shunting several groups out of their accustomed homelands. In about 1815 came the key onslaught. Matiwane of the Ngwane, settled between the upper Bivane and Mfolozi rivers, was just congratulating himself on some judicious alliances with his neighbours when the Ndwandwe hammer fell. The Ngwane were no mere rabbits, however: they had probably been raiding on their own account for a decade. Though they were now badly mauled, they moved away *en masse* and with remarkable cohesion – and descended disastrously on the Hlubi, just to their west. This was famously remembered as 'the shattering of the bottle'.

In the wake of these 'successes', the Ndwandwe felt able to take on even the relatively massive Mthethwa. A series of incursions fell upon, among others, the Zulu. Shaka's forces were first defeated in two clashes near kwaGqokli hill on the White Mfolozi. Another Ndwandwe assault burned the *imizi* of the Zulu heartland to the ground. Shaka had to take the core of his embryonic polity in a wholesale retreat south across the protective Thukela River. This was remembered as a kind of 'scorched earth' withdrawal: crops were burned, grain hidden, cattle driven off to deprive the lightly supplied invaders.

Swimming across the Thukela, Shaka established himself precariously on the border of Qwabe territory, asserting himself over the smaller Maphumulo clan. Then he called on the Qwabe for help. The story of Zulu–Qwabe relations is a complex one, and we'll come back to it in the next chapter. Suffice it to say at this point that, by a judicious mixture of threats, intervention in yet another entangled succession dispute, and no doubt the looming weight of the Mthethwa behind him, Shaka was able to punt his own protégé, Nqetho, into the leadership of the Qwabe. From this base, he could begin to recruit more allies and stiffen his resistance to the Ndwandwe.

Meanwhile, with the lightweight Shaka temporarily out of the way, Zwide turned his attention to the Mthethwa themselves. Apparently unable to quite get the upper hand, Zwide resorted, it's said, to nefarious magic. What happened next is uncertain. Some say Dingiswayo simply marched straight into Zwide's *umuzi*, leaving his *impi* floundering behind. Others say there was something of a fight, in the midst of which he had somehow (being bewitched) wandered off on his own; or he was just sitting apart from the main army, watching the battle from a small hill, when a small Ndwandwe force crept up behind him and nabbed him. There is absolutely no evidence in the traditions that Shaka 'secretly communicated' with the enemy and so betrayed Dingiswayo, as Henry Francis Fynn once alleged.

Dingiswayo's death left a huge leadership vacuum in Mthethwa country. The Mthethwa polity itself quickly disintegrated. Some chose to *khonza* Zwide; some stayed where they were; others fled to Shaka. Shaka saw the succession wrangles beginning and realised he would have to move fast. He had the heir apparent, Mondisa, murdered at a dance, and installed one Mlandela as a willing client-chief.

In 1819 or 1820, the Ndwandwe invaded the Makhosini area. Once again, Shaka was obliged to retreat. But this time he was better prepared. In the vicinity of the Mvuzane stream, where it flows into the Mhlathuze (near present-day Bull's Run, north-west of Eshowe and due south of Melmoth), Shaka had hidden his main force, and waited. Informants differ slightly on details of the approach paths, but everyone is agreed that this is where the decisive fight with Zwide happened.

At around this point, in some accounts, Shaka was busy pumping up his warriors for the assault when an extraordinary thing happened. 'Shaka retired … to the top of a hill and there halted. This was very early. When the sun was about one hour above the horizon, Zwide's *impi* appeared, and advanced towards the heart of the Zulu country. Shaka's men, seeing this, said: "The enemy are in our homes! Let us loose at them!" Shaka sent his force in to the attack. As he was marshalling it, his crane-feather plume came loose from his headband. It fell to the ground, where it stuck in and stood swaying about. His attendants ran to pick it up. The army cried out, "We are full of fear! The king's plume has fallen just as he is sending us out to fight." Shaka said, "Leave it! There is another that will fall." The attendants left it. He said, "Look, Zulu! When you come up to the enemy, if they go up onto the hill and get you down below so that they can attack you from above, leave them." After sending off his force, he told his attendants to fetch the plume. They did so, and he put it back in his headband.'

This is just one of several stories involving that outstanding symbol of Zulu nobility, the blue-crane feather. Maybe there's some less esoteric core-event behind *this* version, something like that related by the informant Baleka: '[Shaka] *took* his crane feather and stuck it in the ground, where it stood swaying …' It's a colourful, retrospective way of saying that Shaka was, as it were, divinely or magically graced. He was powerful enough to turn the omens in his favour.

Feather or no feather, the Zulu triumphed. The armies first made contact through their outrider spies one afternoon, and skirmished. But it was only at dawn the next day that the main clash took place on the Mhlathuze's south bank. It lasted until nightfall, spilling over into the swirling waters. From a nearby hilltop Shaka encouraged his soldiers and vilified the invaders: 'I shall hear, then, men of the elephant. It has come to the home; it has trodden in the excrement of the children.' The Ndwandwe were forced once across the river; they returned; Shaka unleashed the 'black' reserves. That was too much for the Ndwandwe: they fled, to be pursued all the way to Zwide's base at Esikwitshini.

'The bulls of the herd have met,' Shaka is said to have crowed. 'Let the boys who are herding them go out and separate them. Let there go out Noluju [the Ndwandwe *induna*] and Ngqengelele [Shaka's *induna*]. Ha! The one with the red tail [his own *impi*] has gored it! The fancies invented by the Ndwandwe on their way here are finished. They have finished today.'

Apart from the various *amabutho* involved, and one or two stories of individual heroics, we know little more about this most decisive of battles. But it certainly gave Shaka some considerable breathing space in which to begin to consolidate his growing polity from the inside, and to work on forging alliances with other groups further south. (The decisive clash between Shaka and Zwide, as it appears in dozens of museum displays, novels, encyclopaedias and textbooks, is often said to be the 'battle of Qokli Hill'. This was a battle made up by E A Ritter for his novel, *Shaka Zulu*. It never happened.)

As for the defeated Zwide, he was far from being a spent force. The humiliation at the Mvuzane fight was possibly only one factor which made him up stakes and take his main core northwards. Zwide took a sideswipe at Mzilikazi and his Khumalo, roughed up the poor Swazi yet again, but passed even beyond them, retaining enough clout to virtually shatter the Pedi up on the Steelpoort River. There, his son Sikhunyane swore revenge.

The Mvuzane fight excepted, Shaka made no known military ventures north of the Mfolozi rivers in this period (though there may have been light cattle or tribute raids that have been lost to memory). He did not pursue Soshangane or Zwangendaba, former semi-independent client-chiefs of Zwide's, who moved off gradually towards Delagoa Bay, ultimately to set up slaving-states. Though Shaka's name was evidently known at the Bay – he kept up the trade links throughout his reign – he and the Zulu had nothing whatsoever to do with the violence that plagued the region between St Lucia and the lower Phongolo River.

Nor was he really responsible for that other famous southern African wanderer of this period – a man more famous, and less tragic, than Matiwane of the Ngwane: Mzilikazi. Left unexpectedly as leader of his section of the Khumalo after Ndwandwe attacks,

Mzilikazi flirted briefly with becoming tributary to Shaka. The common story that he became a 'general' of Shaka's is rubbish. They did not fight, either. There is a tradition that Shaka tested his loyalty by sending him to extract tribute from some unfortunate group; Mzilikazi, keeping the cattle he was supposed to have given to Shaka, decided to play it safe and move further north. Mzilikazi's movements are obscure until about 1825, when he is found established on the upper Vaal River; from then on, his movements, all the way up to Zimbabwe, were dictated not by Shaka but by the combined assaults of Dingane, slavers, Griqua commandos and Boers.

What Shaka did do was more subtle. He established Maphitha, a man from a strongly related but not genealogically threatening Zulu family, as his client-chief in Ndwandwe territory. Maphitha would rule there, virtually independent, long after Shaka was gone. Some new *imizi* were built, where, as Shaka said, Ndwandwe and others were 'poured together', forming unusual settlements. For the first time, perhaps, major groups were brought into being which were not purely family-based or ethnically unified. In this fashion, Shaka could balance potential power blocs against one another. His half-brother Dingane may have been given some position in this area, too, but we have no details.

This prefigures his strategies in many parts of the central and southern areas of his reach, to which we will now turn.

6

# The limits of control
*Shaka and the south, 1812–1824*

The situation is critical. The northern barbarians have been burning homesteads in the very heart of the motherland. The beaten warriors have been forced to retreat. The *inkosi* must resort to some cunning strategies to enthuse his flagging troops. He gathers them together in the council place of his remaining *umuzi*. He sticks a new and unstained assegai in the dusty ground, points to the north and shouts out, 'There is Zwide, still following me. Let there come forward one Zulu warrior. He who takes this assegai will earn these praises of mine: *The one who was astonished at insults even as he insulted Dlungwana at Embelebeleni!*'

But the warriors are afraid. They think they might be seen as pretending to be equal to the *inkosi* himself. Shaka returns to his seat, invites them to *giya* instead – to dance the war dances, and demonstrate how savagely they will stab.

Hovering at Shaka's elbow is a young *inceku*, a very dark man of medium height. He is a Qwabe. His name is Khomfiya kaNogandaya. Khomfiya had run into trouble among his own people, who lived around the lower reaches of the Mhlathuze, some forty kilometres south of the Zulu. Khomfiya and some chums, climbing over the brow of a hill, had inadvertently spotted some Qwabe princesses cavorting. He and three of his companions were spotted. Rather than be accused of anything, the young men fled – to Shaka. Now, Khomfiya leaps forward and seizes the assegai.

The story of Khomfiya is pivotal in several ways. First, it shows how even in the early years of his reign – even as he was retreating before Zwide's assaults – Shaka was regarded as a potential haven. Shaka, for his part, welcomed with due ceremony such refugees: he needed all the manpower he could get.

Secondly, Khomfiya represents those commoners who could find themselves elevated to substantial positions in the Zulu hierarchy. Hence Shaka has sometimes been represented as astonishingly democratic: a pioneer. That would indeed be astonishing. Although Khomfiya distinguished himself in a series of battles and became an acclaimed hero praise-named as 'Zulu', he was not admitted to the innermost circle: that would still be dominated by elders from the narrowest definition of Zulu-relatedness. This was a thoroughly non-democratic, elitist outgrowth of the conventional social structures, both genealogical and patriarchal.

Thirdly, Khomfiya was a Qwabe: he would become part of the complex politics involved in Shaka's absorption of that substantial group. The Qwabe were probably the first big southern group that Shaka had to cope with. Before he was displaced by Zwide, he had had to deal only with the smaller clans bordering on Zulu country. The first and most obvious of these was the Langeni, his mother's folk. The legend arose that, because he had been so terribly bullied when 'in exile', he lined up the whole Langeni tribe and slaughtered them. It was said that he even tried to fill up the 'Thathiyana Gorge' with the Langeni dead. No one has yet found this gorge, and the tale is clearly nonsense, since the Langeni did *not* disappear. As Shaka asserted his dominance, a few Langeni left, but almost all submitted readily enough.

The same applied to a few other, smaller southern clans. But there was relatively little room to manoeuvre here. Between the Mthlathuze and the Thukela rivers several chunky groups lived: from west to east, the Sithole, the Thembu, the Chunu, the Mkhize and, closest to the coast, the Qwabe. The Mthethwa and Zulu together had a long history of complex relations with these groups, but they had never been able, or had never tried, to assert political dominance over them.

The Qwabe were clearly the main obstacle to any kind of long-term Zulu presence here. Over the years, and especially under their current leader Phakathwayo, the Qwabe had pushed other groups further south, establishing several large *imizi* and boasting some elementary *amabutho*. Shaka initially tried to build an *umuzi* just inside Qwabe land; the Qwabe burned it down; he rebuilt; the Qwabe burned it.

It seems at this point, in retreat from Zwide, Shaka actually asked for help. Phakathwayo snubbed him, with an insult famous in Zulu lore: 'The little Nguni who wears as a penis-cover the fruit-shell used for snuffboxes! Where did he get an *impi* from? Is the *impi* from up-country like the rain? It is nothing but a little string of beads that doesn't even reach the ears.' Naturally Shaka had to avenge his insulted member and somehow managed to attack and kill Phakathwayo, to glorious slaughter.

So goes the story, anyway. There is no solid evidence of such slaughter, but it remains difficult to explain just how the fugitive Shaka got the upper hand and managed to persuade the Qwabe to join forces with him. Almost certainly, Shaka was able to take advantage of simmering internal disputes. With a skilful assassination, in short, and the installation of a viable brother, Nqetho, Shaka was able to bring the Qwabe on side. This was not so much a matter of absorbing the Qwabe as establishing a working partnership, in which Nqetho retained a fair amount of independence.

Even after Zwide's defeat, however, Shaka himself did not move his central base back to the heartland. Perhaps he still felt too insecure; perhaps there were more attractive resources further south. In northern Qwabe country he built first Gibixhegu, then kwaBulawayo, on a prime defensive site on the north-facing escarpment, not far from present-day Eshowe. The white eyewitnesses would subsequently exaggerate the size of this 'capital'; in fact it was, as recent archaeology reveals, about 350 metres across at the widest (the distance between the *isigodlo* at the upper end, to the main entrance gate at the bottom). It contained perhaps 500 huts.

Shaka thoroughly colonised the vicinity of kwaBulawayo, having several *imizi* built, filled with non-Qwabe immigrants. Some *imizi* were known as *amakhanda*, rather too narrowly translated as 'barracks'. These settlements were not just military bases, though they would serve as such for his growing number of *amabutho*. The *amakhanda* were also fully fledged civil establishments, centres for controlling crop production, cattle distribution, training of the youth in all the tasks of both fighting and domestic ritual, and control of women and their marriage alliances. In these central areas, then, Shaka instituted fairly dense control. He also planted some *amakhanda* within the territories of the various client- or partner-chiefs. This was no doubt a way of counterbalancing their relative independence, of being able to keep an eye on things.

Another large group in this southern region would prove to be of similar value to Shaka: the Mkhize, under Zihlandlo kaGcwabe. Nathaniel Isaacs would later meet Zihlandlo at Shaka's 'capital' kwaBulawayo. Zihlandlo was washing Shaka's feet, and Isaacs painted the rather sorry picture of a 'tributary chief' whose 'principal study is to please the savage into whose grasp' he had fallen, 'so as to appease his wrath'. This was far from the truth. A Zulu informant was closer: 'Shaka got Zihlandlo to co-operate with him when building up his power.' Shaka called Zihlandlo his 'younger brother, *mnawe wami*' and promised, 'I will never raid or seize your stock, not to my dying day.' Even when Shaka impulsively picked off a beast of Zihlandlo's, which he thought would make a particularly fine shield, he courteously replaced it.

Shaka would later be blamed for ravaging and depopulating the region south of the Thukela River – the future colony of Natal. But if anyone was ravaging the minor, vulnerable groups in this area, it was the

Mkhize. In time, Mkhize raids would be amplified by those of Zulu *impis*: they worked together. Shaka would arrange, for example, that Zihlandlo exercise some tribute-extracting pressure on a particular clan, sending along a Zulu *induna* to oversee things or a Zulu *impi* for back-up. He kept close tabs on what cattle were captured and where they were lodged: a delicate balance between allowing some independence, distributing resources and rewarding loyalties.

Shaka pursued a different strategy in this region from those he implemented in others. To the north, as we saw, he created another client-chiefdom under Maphitha, one that was almost invented from scratch. In the central region, around the Zulu ancestral heartlands, the area known as Mahlabathini, he caused a dense cluster of new and refurbished *imizi* to be built, thereby reclaiming territories disturbed by the Ndwandwe incursions. By contrast, control of the southern arc was far from outright tyranny. Several client-chiefs did their own thing to a large degree, apparently in willing partnership with Shaka: Jobe of the Sithole, Magaye of the Cele and, furthest away, south of isiBubulungu (as Port Natal or Durban was known to the Zulu), Mathubane of the Thuli. None of these chiefs was ever 'conquered' by Shaka; they joined him because it suited them. In return for greater access to military protection, women and trade goods, they supplied troops and resources specific to their regions. If a chief didn't want to submit to Shaka's tentative over-rule in this way, he simply moved off. The Chunu and the Bhaca, for example, moved sections of their people, along with fragments of other tributary groups, further and further south-west. They were probably prompted as much by raids from Ngwane and displaced Hlubi, and perhaps even by the outriders of slaving expeditions, as they were by Zulu and Mkhize raids. They did not leave in a panic, settled for years at a time in stages, and caused a fair amount of disturbance in their own right.

For Shaka, these 'escapes' were losses, not triumphs. They were diplomatic failures, depriving him of potential allies and manpower. Where he failed diplomatically, he tried judicious military muscle, as in the case of Ngoza's Thembu. That, too, had the opposite of the desired effect: Ngoza moved westwards.

At this stage, his forces were generally reluctant to take on such entities wholesale. No matter how many colourful names his *amabutho* had, no matter what impressively regimented finery they adopted, they were mostly still little more than seasonal raiding parties: some of the *impis* that went out to gather tribute or cattle were no bigger than four men. Most often, as Francis Farewell wrote, attacks were made swiftly and at night. This swiftness suited both the deployment of smaller forces and the kind of political impact Shaka sought. He was not seeking widespread destruction, only widespread respect. As one informant put it: 'Shaka did not put to death the [chieftains] he defeated if, when he proceeded against them, they ran away and did not show fight. He made them *izinduna*.' In just one example, Kutshwayo of the Dube, 'like many others, was attacked merely to make him pay tribute, to reduce him to become a subject and then instate him as an *induna*'. In short, 'Shaka's policy at first was to attack one tribe at a time and take care not to embroil others. He would take special pains to warn adjoining tribes that he was not attacking them in any way, and so his enemies would be reduced to clearly defined limits.' At every level, the use of military terror was to be highly selective. Nathaniel Isaacs confirms these Zulu testimonies: 'It is not the Zoolas' system of warfare to meet their enemy openly, if they can avoid it: they like to conquer by stratagem, and not by fighting, and to gain by a ruse what might be difficult for them to achieve by the spear.' It was rare, in fact, that open battle *couldn't* be avoided.

One final point about Shaka and tactics: Shaka never personally fought in the raids and seldom directed the details of tactics on the ground. As Farewell noted, Shaka 'never goes with the army himself but remains generally five or six days in the rear ... so that he never incurs any personal risk.' This was only sensible, and it makes nonsense of the common myth that 'Shaka himself took shield and arms and with his own hand killed people'. Excepting Shaka's apprenticeship under Dingiswayo, there is no evidence for this whatsoever.

Nor were Shaka's raiders always successful. The evidence is plentiful that many of the small groups had to be pummelled repeatedly, to renew their protection payments, as it were. These smaller entities, squeezed between the larger ones, did begin to feel the crunch in the early 1820s. Under the impact of combined Mkhize and Zulu raids, a brief 'confederacy' coalesced to try to punch through the southern ring of heftier chiefdoms. This they did, but ran up against the sturdy Mpondo on the Mzimvubu River and were sent scattering north-east again.

The myth is powerful that in some paradisal era fighting was light, mannered and largely bloodless; then Shaka came along and abruptly transformed the region into a bloodbath of 'total war'. However, in only a few very restricted areas did stereotypical mayhem break out, involving the destruction of homes and the murder of women and children. And that was aberrant.

Most of the so-called depopulation of the Natal sector, between the Thukela and Mngeni rivers, appears to have been the work of one particular unit. This was the mostly Hlubi iziYendane *ibutho*, so named after the swaying of their tell-tale dreadlocks. Composed largely of refugees from the 'shattering-of-the-bottle' attack who had sought shelter under Shaka, they were by now hardened and not a little footloose. They had been dispatched across the Thukela to sow some judicious terror with their red shields. They got completely out of hand. For a year or more, the iziYendane ravaged settlements south of the Thukela until Shaka disbanded them, executing some of the ringleaders and scattering the remainder. It was no doubt the skeletal remains of iziYendane raids that alarmed the first white visitors, on their way from isiBubulungu to kwaBulawayo in 1824. Even then, the destruction had been patchy: on the very next ridge, they'd find more densely populated areas, with well-tended crops. Moreover, there is almost no evidence for this kind of thing happening anywhere else in Shaka's sphere of influence.

By 1824, then, Shaka had established fairly tight control over a quite restricted area stretching from Nhlazatshe in the north to kwaBulawayo in the south – an area not more than a hundred kilometres long, maybe half as wide. Outside that, Shaka exercised varying degrees of indirect rule. This was either through client-chiefs, most of whom retained considerable autonomy and authority to run crucial rituals, execute wrongdoers and distribute women through their own *izigodlo*; or through sporadic and persistent raids, which probably were generally little more than periodic annoyances to the recipients.

Force was always present, of course, the tool of initial or final resort. However, Shaka ought to be better known for a portfolio of other methods of ruling a growing polity, methods both more subtle and more interesting than merely beating people about the head with a knobkierie.

7

# The nature of the state

'He finally succeeded in establishing a sort of *Zoolacratical* form of government, (if I may so term it, for I do not know of anything resembling it in either ancient or modern history), a form that defies description or detail; that can neither be comprehended nor digested, and such a one as gives protection to no living creature …' That is Nathaniel Isaacs, laying the foundation for the stereotypical view of Shaka's polity: unique, terroristic, fundamentally incomprehensible; in a word, uncivilised. Happily, we've come a long way from that. Great distortion persists, but even for an outsider to Zulu society, a deeper understanding is now quite readily available.

Isolating 'the nature of the state' in a separate chapter like this threatens a certain distortion of its own. There has long been a tendency to write dynamic (usually military) *history* separately from static (domestic) *society*. Books about early southern

Africa have habitually begun with a chapter about 'precolonial society' as if it were some eternally changeless thing – an 'ethnographic present' populated by 'an aimless people, happy and careless, with little sense of time and less of purpose', as the American historian Donald Morris put it in his famous (and profoundly misleading) book, *The Washing of the Spears*. This 'Black Man's Arcady', as Bryant called it, would then erupt into chronologically mobile, furious and documented 'history': Chapter Two. In the case of the early Zulu, Shaka has usually been portrayed as the solitary, self-created, explosive force which disrupted the idyll forever. So the first thing we must emphasise is that, either before or under Shaka, the 'nature of the state' was changing rapidly all the time, even as it rested on crucial continuities with the past.

The second thing to emphasise is that there was no secure division between the fighter and the cattle-owner, between the warrior and the husband, in Zulu society. Some institutions appear to be 'military' only because other functions of those same formations have been ignored. Chroniclers of every hue prefer to talk about blood-stirring heroism rather than weeding. But in fact, because campaigning happened only seasonally, for a few weeks each year, the leading men or *izinduna* would spend the bulk of their time performing civic and domestic functions: supervising crops and marriages, building cattle-posts, regulating trade and justice. The *amakhanda* certainly functioned as 'barracks' for the *amabutho* and their developing warrior ethic. But for most of the year they functioned as centres for domestic activities.

A third problem to bear in mind is the very definition of the 'state'. It has always been assumed that Shaka was building up a *state*. A state (usually) is highly centralised, hierarchically arranged, and geographically coherent; it has unified judicial systems and a standing army; it has *size*. The archaeologist Martin Hall has suggested the term is too loose to be of much use in Shaka's context. I'd say it's too tight. Therefore I've preferred to use the term 'polity', which in a way is even looser, but it evades at least some inappropriate preconceptions.

As we've seen, by 1824, when Shaka was hitting his stride in terms of organisation, the Zulu sphere of influence wasn't unified at all. It was constantly threatening to break up, since its individual segments retained strong attachments to their separate identities. In fact, when Shaka died, it *did* break up – and broke up repeatedly over the next century. And as we've also noted, Shaka's strategies by necessity varied from one sector of his sphere to another: there is no *one* 'state' to possess a 'nature'. Mostly, this chapter will focus on that small area which Shaka most directly controlled.

*This is the proof for a woodcut print by the South African Cecil Skotnes, destined for his dramatic collection* The Assassination of Shaka *(1973), accompanied by poems by Stephen Gray. It depicts Shaka's engagement with his 'court of justice', or iqoqo. (Image courtesy of Pippa Skotnes)*

Certain things not even Shaka could control: the weather and the seasons. Above all else, this agriculturally dependent people needed to feed their stomachs. This meant access to water, grazing for cattle, and – even more importantly – arable soils for their grains. Though cattle were the primary form of visible wealth, they were less often eaten than displayed. Most people ate sorghum and vegetables, supplemented with some hunting. This meant that even a single disrupted season could spell hardship. It limited where people could viably live; it made some areas more attractive than others.

Shaka had to operate within these environmental constraints. Most of his strategies of control, then, revolved around food supplies, not assegais. The latter could, of course, often be used to gain the former; but it was much more complex than that. As already shown, Shaka's basic policy was to assimilate people or at least cajole or bully them into partnership or a condition of regular tribute. 'Conquered' or assimilated people would then give over to central control some of their surplus in grain, cattle, women, fighting men or other specialised resources like iron or monkey-skins or lourie feathers. Women were a vital bargaining chip.

This wasn't strictly new. It was developed out of the long-established *ukwethula* system, which involved the obligation by any family's junior house to transfer the eldest daughter to the senior house in return for cattle or other payment. The richer a man, the more such women dependants he could attract. They would be brought up in the household as *umdlunkulu*, his to dispose of in marriage as he pleased. Shaka simply extended the range. Since the richest men were those increasingly patronised by Shaka, and they were generally of the closest collateral clans, they got a lot of young women to exchange for *lobolo*, as did Shaka himself. In this way wealth – mostly expressed in cattle, secondarily in beads – also became more centralised and elitist.

The *umdlunkulu* were housed in the *isigodlo*, the almost sacrosanct enclosure at the head of the settlement. It was labyrinthine, topped with thorny *ugagane* branches. Some of these *umdlunkulu* women would enjoy considerable status, using their own entrances and paths, eating certain choice parts of a beast. They were distinguished by particular ornaments: girdles of *umbedle* leaves, large red and green beads around the loins and strung from the ears, brass *isongo* rings on their arms. The *amakhosikazi*, those closest to the *inkosi*, were marked by heavy brass neck-rings and arm-bangles. They grew fat as pigs, groused one informant; they made the mats wet where they sat. When they went to the river to wash they would be accompanied by armed men, and if you chanced upon them you had to fall flat on your face in respect.

Most of the *isigodlo* women, however, were little more than captives – *izinqila* – who had to work hard carrying wood, tending crops, carrying chamberpots. Their labour was vital to the health of the whole establishment, to be guarded against both abduction and sexual abuse. Hence the *isigodlo* was a good place for the *inkosi* himself to shelter. His person, too, had to be protected against both actual invasion (like assassination attempts) and magical malpractice. In particular, the *inkosi*'s bodily emissions – faeces, hair shavings, semen, spittle – had to be carefully contained and disposed of. Urine was caught in a calabash and carried away by a small girl. The most basic functions of the *inkosi*'s life were carefully regulated, even ritualised, by the select staff of the *isigodlo*.

The *isigodlo* was architecturally adorned in special ways. The young Charles Rawden Maclean was once able to take a peek. 'We observed before us another gateway in the side of the square, fronting the one by which we entered, that leads to another oblong enclosure, more spacious than the former, and containing a dozen or more huts, still more elegant of construction and of still larger dimensions. The floor of this enclosure is of glassy smoothness, with a polish that reflects the image like a mirror. A continuation of enclosures of this last description, with more or less huts in them, and of different shapes, some semi-circular and some triangular, which together complete the internal economy.' The *isigodlo* was, therefore, where the most important decisions were made, and few could enter. (The fact that the 1824 assassination attempt was made within the wooden gates of the *isigodlo* strongly indicates that it must have been an 'inside job'.)

From the hub of the *isigodlo*, the *inkosi* would regulate the ritual life of the country. Shaka centralised his control of agricultural resources by appropriating the major rituals. The *inkosi* was responsible for conducting rain-making ceremonies, with the help of specialised rain-summoners, *izinyanga*. He also commanded the *umkhosi* 'first-fruits' ceremony, the major agricultural event of the year. Gradually he was able to dictate over a considerable area who could or could not conduct such rituals: it was a mark of singular favour if you were allowed your own *isigodlo* or your own *umkhosi* ceremony.

This went intimately with rewarding certain families over others, either with cattle or with land. Certain commoners and outsiders could make their way through the ranks or penetrate the inner council. (That there *was* a council, or *isiqoqo*, is almost entirely ignored in the history: Shaka probably made few decisions entirely alone.) The council was the preserve almost exclusively of family insiders, close relatives of the various collateral branches.

These 'blood' relationships and genealogies were capable of some massaging. Even at this level the principle of exogamy – marrying outside the immediate clan – held true. The drive to centralise was offset by the tendency to split away. Shaka was able to turn this to his advantage. Basically, there were two ways in which a new, expanding family could split off to form a new clan: *dabuka* ('to get torn off') and *dabula* ('to tear off'). *Dabuka* was usually meant to achieve an independent political existence for the section concerned. It would be led away to build a new settlement elsewhere, but it would remain tied to the parent section by retaining its praises or *izibongo*. *Dabula*, on the other hand, involved the new section creating additional *izibongo* of its own; it might move no further away geographically, but intermarriage would thereafter be permissible.

In Shaka's day, new clans were *dabula*'d with unusual frequency. Shaka was trying to confine political clout to a limited number of family branches by encouraging greater inbreeding. Some *dabula*'d clans then fabricated genealogies to give the impression that they had originated separately. They could intermarry but were no direct threat to the *inkosi*, since, as Carolyn

Hamilton writes, being 'no longer "Zulu" [in terms of their *isibongo*], they lacked the crucial abilities of the Zulu proper to intervene … on behalf of the nation … in the heavens as the source of rain, and in the control of lightning'.

It's difficult to draw boundaries between these clans, partly because they were already so closely interrelated, partly because they were still in the process of forming. It was still a very shadowy, muddled process. We also lack sufficient detail about who got married off to whom, to map the whole process clearly enough.

Still, it's clear that a parallel system of elite leaders – *izinduna* – was being laid across the existing networks of local family authorities. An *induna* might be rewarded with cattle plundered in a raid, a wife or two from the *isigodlo*, and some land in the vicinity of a new *ikhanda* built by the men he commanded within 'foreign' territory: Cele country, say, or the former Mthethwa-controlled region. Those men themselves might come from somewhere else altogether, without any distracting local attachments.

The granting of land worked something like this: 'The land of Zululand belongs to Shaka, he who unified all of it. Shaka would take a fancy to a man and then, having conquered some chief's land, would say this man might go and build at any spot Shaka might indicate … The old resident would not be called upon to quit. If, later on, a quarrel were to arise, it might end in the two going to Shaka, who would generally cause the old resident to move to some other locality … Those who were conquered were not required to ask permission to remain. There was no necessity; they merely continued to occupy as before.' Hence, there was no real reason for Shaka to assign boundaries, which 'were determined by the *izizwe* (tribes) defeated, i.e. the lands occupied by them'. On both the small scale and the large, 'boundaries' would remain very fluid, marked if at all by rivers and hills.

Some *izinduna*, having been granted the authority to dispense cattle, arm their men, gather tribute, get the crops in and occasionally punish wrongdoers with death (another rare privilege), might throw their weight around a little. As one informant wryly noted, the *izinduna* 'masked many [genuine] heroes through mere self-seeking. A hero who had killed maybe 3 or 4 would be silenced by its being said by the *izinduna* that some other man, some special favourite (like a prince) had killed a couple of the very men named …' This could border on uncontrollable abuse. 'It was the *izinduna* who were responsible for the indiscriminate killing off that went on. Sometimes a man rewarded with cattle by the king would be killed just as he reached his home, and his cattle seized. These cattle … would be taken off to the *izinduna*'s kraals, and they would report that nothing in the shape of cattle was at the kraal.' In short, the *izinduna* were an elite. They showed off their status with displays of brass bangles, beads and particular birds' feathers, which the *inkosi* supplied for the purpose. In this way they distinguished themselves from the petty chieftains and headmen, who remained where they were on the land, paying tribute to the new authorities when obliged to.

Little wonder, then, that Shaka also tried to offset the power of the *izinduna* by placing the major *amakhanda* under the oversight of especially powerful women – Mnkabayi, Langazana, his own mother Nandi – who had considerable influence but were not direct genealogical threats to the *inkosi*. They were a crucial element in the delicate checks and balances Shaka was setting up.

If the ostentation of brass adornments and fancy beadwork was one 'language' of elite power, verbal language was another. Shaka's ability to wield linguistic propaganda seems to have been both cunning and far-reaching. We've already mentioned the ways in which genealogies could be 'rewritten' to assert common origins. Praise-names, or *ithakazelo*, could also be newly applied to suggest a new, common identity. So the term *ntungwa*, for example, came to be used by a number of disparate groups to indicate that they had all originated 'up-country', which is to say, with the

Zulu ruling class. Related terms – Nguni, Lala – were similarly manipulated. As a Cele informant attested: 'Shaka ... used to insult us [Cele] and frighten us by saying that we did not have the cunning to invent things out of nothing, like lawyers ... He said that we were Lala because our tongues lay (*lala*) flat in our mouths, and we did not speak in the Ntungwa fashion. He spoke of them as iNyakeni because they had dirty habits and did not distinguish between what was good and what was bad ... nor did he wash or keep himself neat ... These names Lala and Nyakeni may have been and probably were in existence long before Shaka's day, but it was in his day that they came to be widely known.' Some peoples even worked to alter their dialects to conform to the rulers': as happens everywhere, this is a ticket to greater acceptance. Such changes weren't necessarily enforced but would happen as a natural consequence of shifts in power relations.

On the one hand, then, Shaka worked to institute a new language of belonging which cut across former, fragmentary clan or ethnic identities. This would be the foundation for the consciousness of a Zulu 'nation' as it continued to evolve under Shaka's successors. At the same time, he popularised, or even institutionalised, terms of abuse for outsiders. Within the society itself, he encouraged other divisions between the elite and the commoners. The trappings of wealth associated with the *umdlunkulu* women and the *izinduna* were amplified by those granted to the *amabutho*, with increasingly ornate ceremonial finery and colourful praise-names ringing with competitive pride. The iNtontela *ibutho*, for instance, was granted the name 'Amehlakamboni' as a praise-name 'given after something good or worthy done in war'.

Importantly, Shaka also extended another common linguistic practice, that of *hlonipha*. This complex phenomenon essentially involved tabooing a word that had acquired a disrespectful echo. It was said, for example, that Shaka *hlonipha*'d the word *itshaka* – the intestinal disease snidely alleged by some to have been the cover for Nandi's pregnancy – and replaced it with *iqagane* or *iqangala*.

What is surprising to us now, perhaps, is that none of this depended on a system of internal terror, arbitrary murders or mass destruction of cowards. There was little of that. Make no mistake: they were brutal times, and people died in brutal ways. But the polity came together as much through the propaganda of belonging as by compulsion. It's not possible to say this with certainty, but I wouldn't mind betting that throughout his reign Shaka sentenced to death fewer people than the 269 executed by the state of Texas during the governorship of George W Bush.

# 8

# The nature of the man

Despite himself, Henry Francis Fynn penned one of the more measured assessments of Shaka's character. '[Shaka] was inflexible in his resolves severe in his discipline and the terror of his enemies. Of the soldiery notwithstanding his atrocities he was the Idol and to a conquered enemy where he had no suspicion of witchcraft he was liberal and lenient. The sacred character of Embassadrie from his most inveterate enemie even in the [ardour?] of the conflict he always respected and ensured their safety. To the brave he was liberal to an excess, to the cowardly merciless and cruel. Vain, haughty, imperious, and cruel to his subjects, to the Europeans he was affable, and kind, anxious to know all their wants only to alleviate them, possessing a perpetual thirst for knowledge which he received with caution, and conversed, with a shrewdness and policy which would not have disgraced many civilized beings …'

As we have seen, Fynn's writings need to be read with caution. But those phrases, 'liberal and lenient', 'sacred character of Embassadrie', 'affable and kind', have largely been lost in a flood of allegations of unbridled savagery. They lie uneasily alongside the epithets of Shaka's haughtiness, his 'terror' and his 'atrocities', and Fynn felt it necessary to explain this 'opposite character' as an inherent mystery: 'Such opposed kinds of conduct in one person appeared to me to be strange, but I afterwards became convinced that both the contradictory dispositions, delicate feeling and extreme brutality, were intimately blended in him.' While we all recognise that people can be oddly contradictory, and would (as every novelist knows) be extremely uninteresting if they weren't, this does not take us very far.

One would love to be able to sum up and *explain* this most illustrious man, to find some sort of 'key' to his personality, and to write a proper 'biography'. But we will have to admit, I think, that the material on which to base one doesn't exist. We have a limited number of dubious anecdotes from more or less dubious sources. The white traders spent very little time with Shaka, obviously misunderstood a lot of what they did see, and then tried to lie and exaggerate their way out of trouble. The Zulu sources are equally problematic, most of them recorded in dangerously long retrospect, and riddled with malicious stories put about by Dingane or other enemies. We have no information about his childhood sufficient to explain his adult psychology; we have no unmediated testimony from his own perspective. We do not even know what he looked like: one informant thought he was short, very dark, and broad-bottomed; another that he was lighter-skinned with the taut buttocks of a dancer. Some Zulu recalled only an excessively sweaty nose that 'sat on his face like a toad'. The whites never bothered to describe him at all. In sum, we *know* next to nothing.

A few things I think we can safely say Shaka was *not*. He was not a pathological mass murderer. He did not slaughter large numbers of cowards; he did not order the wholesale killing of women, children and dogs; he did not hurl people off the cliffs at Shaka's Rock or anywhere else; he did not obliterate the Langeni or any other group. He did not kill his own mother.

I am not trying to whitewash Shaka. Not even his admirers said he was warm and cuddly. He could hardly have become the regional leader he was, had he not been uncompromisingly tough, wily and adept. As with governments everywhere, his edicts were in the last resort enforced, sometimes by brutal and fatal methods. (In England at the same time, a man could be hanged at Newgate for stealing a loaf of bread.) He had

*The Kenyan writer Meja Mwangi's novel is just one of many reworkings of the Shaka figure as liberator, almost a force of nature who reincarnates as African saviour. (Note the automatic rifle slung over Shaka's shoulder.)*

people executed. He was expected to. As one informant said blithely: '[Shaka] was always talking of war. He snuffed a good deal. The old regime was good, even though the king killed off frequently. We used to think the king was having sport and we thought but little of it. He never seemed in earnest.' This was doubtless of little comfort to those whose necks were being broken or were suffering stakes hammered into the anus, in the fashion of the day. It's equally unsurprising that others were less accepting. 'That man used to play around with people,' said one informant. And another: 'Shaka did not hold trials, he simply killed people off.' He was called 'the wrongdoer who knows no law', and 'the violently unrestrained one'.

There is, however, little evidence that his acts disregarded traditional law altogether. It seems much more likely that at least most of the killings which the whites observed (as opposed to the massacres they *claimed* happened but did *not* observe) were done for traditionally sanctioned political or judicial ends. To Charles Maclean, Shaka once explained 'very seriously': '"if it was not for me I fear there is scarcely an umfogasann [*umfokozana*] (a common man, or an expression of the lower order of the natives) but would rejoice of having the opportunity to kill my white people. Oh!" he continued, "they are a bad people; I am obliged to kill a few to gratify the rest; and if I were not to do it, they would think me an old woman, a coward, and kill me themselves."'

Maclean was sympathetic to both Shaka and the Zulu as a people. Even he didn't minimise Shaka's executions but felt that many of them were not Shaka's doing alone. They were 'prompted by degrading superstitions' or 'at the instance of a cringing and cowardly scoundrel named Mbopha, a confidential servant'. (An interesting snippet, given Mbopha's role in Shaka's eventual assassination.) Maclean, though 'far from vindicating cruelties, with many of which Shaka can be justly charged', vehemently denied the genocidal allegations that appeared, for instance, in the missionary Stephen Kay's *Travels and Researches in Kaffraria* (1833). Kay, despite being keen to rubbish the Port Natal traders' reputations, was happy to regurgitate the stories spun by James Saunders King of mass murder of whole regiments and of 170 children killed off 'before breakfast'. These 'monstrous absurdities', Maclean fumed, 'supplied either by the fertility of the writer's brain or from exaggerated and evil report', were a 'monstrous injustice'.

The same can be said of the many febrile accusations made about Shaka's allegedly deviant sexuality. Shaka had tried to control the question of his own succession by not getting married – or at least, after his sojourn with the Mthethwa, not getting married again. This peculiarity would spawn a whole gamut of theories that he was abnormal. The anthropologist Max Gluckman speculated that he was impotent; the historian Donald Morris trumpeted that he was 'unquestionably a latent homosexual'. This is rank nonsense. If anything, the sources make him out to be sexually predatory. He did not remarry for political reasons; he did not want sons to contest his leadership, as sons (including himself) had a tendency to do. It seems fairly certain that he *did* have children. Occasional lovers apparently fell pregnant and aborted the foetuses with conventional medicines. Some children may yet have survived and been farmed out to live in relative obscurity. So said Charles Maclean, anyway; he mentioned he had actually met one or two of these offspring.

We can likewise dump other stories that were demonstrably transferred from Dingane to Shaka. For example, some of Stuart's informants blamed Shaka for the murder of one of his own favourite client-chiefs, Mathubane of the Thuli, but it is abundantly clear from other sources that it was Dingane. The infamous story of Shaka 'feeding the vultures' with his victims seems also to have been deflected from Dingane.

The most notorious atrocity story of all was probably spread by Dingane. This was the story that Shaka once cut open a pregnant woman 'to see how the foetus lay'. It's hard to say whether there is any core of truth to this. It might have had its origin in an abortion performed on one of Shaka's accidentally impregnated mistresses. It might have begun with another alleged incident, in which a woman was executed for being particularly nasty to Shaka, and he had her cut open to see what kind of heart such a cruel woman might possess. In certain fevered imaginations, what *might* have been a single incident got multiplied; it became a 'policy'; it amounted to hundreds; it included a wife or wives of Dingane's, and this is why Dingane killed him. In this sequence, we can trace pretty conclusively the story's progression from a single rumour, through a more general accusation, to Dingane's obvious self-justification.

So we must at least suspect that a number of the other negative stories were also spread by Dingane. Very few incidents of outright cruelty were unambiguously or verifiably witnessed within Shaka's lifetime. At least some can be said to have some judicial basis, even if they were undeniably unpleasant, like the fate of the cattle-thief Gcugcwa. Shaka strapped him down across a cattle enclosure's gate and had the herd that Gcugcwa 'was so enamoured of' run over him. As for the rest, a thorough trawling of both white and Zulu sources reveals, at most, a couple of dozen more *alleged* incidents. The other stories that are pretty familiar are fiction.

Are the recorded incidents of cruelty just the tip of an iceberg – or themselves exaggerations? It is difficult not to feel that there's *some* grain of truth in them. If anything comes through, it's that Shaka had a definite sense of humour, but one barbed with a certain malice. He enjoyed frightening the whites by pretending they were about to be charged by buffalo or by giving them pieces of ironwood on which he knew perfectly well their nails and gimlets would break. When presented with strange medicines, he tried them out on people in exuberant quantities, with apparent delight at the ugly results. Yet, despite the whites' sneering, nothing is more evident in these conversations than Shaka's intense intelligence. He was robust and perceptive in his criticism of the whites' practices of jailing people, wearing shoes, having pale skins, even of their weapons.

There are similarly malicious stories in the Zulu sources, too. Shaka was famous for playing a trick on one of his *amabutho*, the iziMpohlo. He allowed them to go off and *soma* with their girls: 'They put on their finery, and scattered; not one of them remained. They disappeared completely. Shaka said, "Hau! How empty the place is! Where has everyone gone?" "Au, Nkosi, there is not a single man left." "So they went off when they heard my order? So, in spite of my prohibition they still want the girls?" "Au, Father, there is not a single one of them left." "Weu! Let a force go out to eat them up." … The force ate up their cattle. After this had happened a man of the Izimpohlo came forward and said, "Our cattle have been eaten up. We were given the order deliberately; it was he who gave us permission to go and *soma*."'

The temerity of the iziMpohlo in querying the decision apparently 'frightened Shaka'. His response was to slaughter their cattle; none were returned. The man who had first uttered the fateful question fled, turning at the brow of the hills and shouting back, 'The destructiveness of the Zulu people has risen up against them!' In these later retellings, what was perhaps a way of reducing a unit's overweening arrogance is turned inaccurately into an example of wayward destructiveness.

Another well-known trick almost certainly had more pragmatic political motives: the occasion when Shaka is said to have sprinkled blood about his doors and gateposts, and then called on various *izinyanga*, medicine men, to 'smell out' who had done it. Those who divined wrongly were killed off. Though there is absolutely no reason to think that Shaka did not subscribe fully to the spiritual beliefs of his people, this obvious set-up may have been an occasion to get rid of certain over-powerful individuals – even to get at his own brothers, already plotting to be rid of him. There are, however, so many versions of the story that it's impossible to say now what might have been at the root of it.

Another comment of Fynn's is interesting here: 'In their haste a group of men passed within five yards of Shaka, not having noticed him till they got to within that distance. He looked upon them so fiercely as to make them run back, whereupon he vociferated his usual oath, "*Mnkabayi!*" in so violent a manner as to bring them to a momentary stand. He then ordered an attendant to single out a man and stab him … The moment the assegai pierced the body Shaka averted his head, his countenance betraying something like a feeling of horror, but we had not proceeded more than a mile when two other unfortunates experienced the same fate.' At any rate, this is how it appeared in *The Diary of Henry Francis Fynn*. The editor James Stuart, however, emended Fynn's rather less eloquent original notes, omitting the crucial phrase 'as an example', which makes Shaka's political and disciplinary logic clearer.

If punishments may be said to have had political motives, even if they caused Shaka some remorse, the same may be said of his generosities. Nevertheless, for every story of an apparently arbitrary execution, we have one in which someone is well treated. Perhaps the best we can do now is to balance the tales of sadistic cruelty against an almost equal number of surviving tales of generosity and judicious balance. These more positive stories have all but been lost from sight.

For example, one man was about to be executed for concocting evil medicines against an elder. Shaka asked him which were the most delightful things he regretted leaving behind. The wretch replied, 'I leave the king whom merely to converse with face to face is an inexpressible delight; next, the smile of a little child that has just learnt to sit up by itself; and lastly, the young shoot of a mealie plant, to look on which is enchanting, especially when seen with one's head brought so as to view the tops of a whole field.' Pleased with the compliment or the poetry, Shaka let him off.

Once, Shaka is said to have encountered a woman in an appalling state of filth and destitution. Shaka demanded who her husband was, giving her some calves to set her right. When the miscreant husband presented himself, he was upbraided for his neglect – though once he'd praised the *inkosi*, he too was released.

How much this was mere appeal to vanity is hard to say. The whites made much mileage of the fact that a self-obsessed Shaka wanted macassar oil to hide his greying hairs, going so far as to imply that the whole of state policy became subordinated to this 'absurd nostrum', as Isaacs called it. The contemporary documentation makes clear, however, that the oil was only one of a range of medicinal supplies that Shaka sought and was of much less importance than firearms, dogs, letter-writing equipment and wax seals.

Shaka regularly rewarded bravery and athleticism. He spared defeated enemies wherever they were no longer an obvious threat. As Maclean wrote: 'The policy of adding these brave men to his band of warriors, to strengthen and promote his success in future schemes of conquest, might be considered as the primary and only motive in the savage chief for exercising the act of mercy, were it not known that courage always had been a sure passport to Shaka's favour and esteem.'

For several years he supported the emergent white settlements, supplying them regularly with cattle and workers, allowing them to establish themselves in return for quite customary specified services. As their own writings make abundantly clear, the whites had no reason whatsoever to doubt Shaka's generosity, however unnerved they might have been by his vigorous treatment of his own miscreants. Their subsequent vilification of him was an ungrateful response to all he had done for them.

In sum, little of what has been said about Shaka can be accepted without qualification. Tough he unquestionably was, seldom if ever gratuitously cruel, frequently generous, sharply intelligent, a touch vain but not immune to criticism, humorous but sometimes nastily so – someone looked upon and remembered with mingled respect and nervous but grateful awe. As his *izibongo* proclaimed, Shaka was 'He who armed in the forest, who is like a madman' and 'Spear that is red even on the handle', but he was also 'a pile of rocks at Nkandla, which was a shelter for the elephants in bad weather'.

9

# Black in all other respects
*Shaka and the white visitors, 1824–1828*

'Shaka, on the occasion of his first Pondo *impi*, crossed at the Point, Durban. He struck the water and it divided into two, and he and his regiments crossed over. He crossed to the Bluff and thence along the ridges to Mpunyungwana hill, below the Sipingo and between the Mlazi and Zimbodoko streams, where he slept.' A story of wonderful biblical echoes, reminding us that so-called oral testimonies are by no means uncontaminated by foreign literary influences.

The first campaign against the Mpondo, living a hundred kilometres or so south of isiBubulungu, was launched in the dry season of 1824. You will recall that by this time Shaka was firmly established at Gibixhegu/ kwaBulawayo. In the north he had defeated his main rival, Zwide of the Ndwandwe; some other potentially threatening groups like the Khumalo had moved away; and he had begun consolidating the Zulu heartlands. South of the Mhlathuze and partly south of the

Thukela, Shaka was relying on a string of client-chiefs. Only the Mthethwa and the Qwabe could be said to have been 'incorporated' to any great extent; the rest were in willing, if somewhat subordinate, partnership with the Zulu potentate.

For the first time, after some twelve years of rule, Shaka felt confident enough to launch a long-distance raid. He aimed to plunder cattle from the well-established and relatively prosperous Mpondo people living around the Mzimvubu River, in the vicinity of present-day Port St Johns. This might have been the start of extracting more regular tribute from them, too, or extending his client-chief base.

The raid was a failure. 'The army crossed the Thukela into Natal well above Greytown ... skirted along the Drakensberg range ... travelled southwards, sweeping round, slightly entered Mpondo territory, and made its way along the coast back to Zululand, crossing the Mzimkulu in the neighbourhood of Port Shepstone ... The force then entered Pondoland, coming to Manci's territory (a Pondo *induna*). They merely affected [*sic*] an entrance and made a slight seizure of cattle. The Pondos came to the attack. The Pondos *sika*'d – stabbed – three regiments. Seeing this, Mdhlaka reinforced the three regiments being defeated [with] youths, and got the better of the Pondos. After this the Zulus came back homewards.'

The forces, which were not terribly substantial in the first place, seriously miscalculated the distance, the hardship and perhaps the stiffness of Mpondo resistance. They came away with so few cattle that they were forced to eat melons – *amabece* – filched from homesteads along the route. From then on, it was known as the *amabece* campaign.

On their way home, they crossed the very beach where now sprawls the complex named (in what must rank as the most ironic invention in the history of South African tourism) uShaka Marine World. There they apparently encountered what for many of them was their first white man. It was Henry Francis Fynn. Typically, Fynn later depicted a stupendous army which in all its finery took hours to pass. In reality it must have been a rather bedraggled and dispirited bunch.

Fynn had just spent several months in Delagoa Bay, meeting Captain W F W Owen, who, under the cover of a coastal surveying expedition, was forging treaties with local chiefs in order to oust the Portuguese. Fynn then teamed up with Francis Farewell, James Saunders King and some other Cape Town speculators, making a number of landings at St Lucia and at isiBubulungu, which they called Port Natal. They had made a start on extracting ivory and maybe slaves, though they were just a little hapless: one landfall at St Lucia collapsed into a tragi-comic series of capsizes, drownings, fisticuffs and at least one escaped prisoner.

Fynn, Farewell and associated 'businessmen' met Shaka for the first time in early 1825. From that moment on, they would portray themselves as the centre of attention and action, overawing the ignorant natives with their horses, firearms and medicines. In fact, it was they who were overawed. As Farewell wrote, 'The king received us surrounded by a large number of his chiefs and about eight or nine thousand armed men, observing a state and ceremony on our introduction that we little expected, and his subjects appeared to treat him with such submission and respect as to rank him far above any chiefs I believe known in South Africa, whilst the nation he governs in manners, customs and mode of ornamenting themselves are so different from any hitherto known as to at once astonish and please us ... I fancy [Shaka] assembled all his disposable force on the occasion of our visit and probably fifty thousand souls, fourteen of which might be fighting men on a push, forms *the whole population of the large territory he is possessed of.*'

Farewell's sober estimate would be overwhelmed by Fynn's and Isaacs's subsequent exaggerations. Nor would Fynn admit to the awkward humiliation recorded by one Zulu informant: 'Shaka said, "Hear, my people! Magaye says the white men have arrived in his country." He presently noticed the white object among them. He gave the bystanders various orders as regards making the white man do this and that. He took it into his head to cause the white man to undress and put on his, Shaka's, loin-cover, which was fetched from his hut. Having a sense of decency, Shaka ordered 30 or 40 men to stand round about the white man so as to hide him while he undressed. This was done, and Fynn presently appeared in the garb of a Zulu, his flesh as white as milk.' This set the trend for the future. The whites tried to conceal most of what they got up to, misunderstood much of what they saw, and exaggerated the rest. They claimed to be morally pure, to have rescued thousands of refugees from Shaka's ferocity, to have prevented him from committing further atrocities.

In fact they became more of a tool in Shaka's broader ambitions. They were out on a limb and beholden, and were left in no doubt about this fact. To their surprise, when they arrived at kwaBulawayo for the first time, they came face to face with none other than the ex-Robben Island convict, Xhosa sheep-stealer Jacob Msimbithi – the very prisoner who had run away at St Lucia a year before. He was known here as Hlambamanzi – 'Swim-the-Seas' – and was already well set up with his own *umuzi* and wives. He would continue his extraordinary, boundary-crossing career as an interpreter between Shaka and the whites, and would eventually be shot in cold blood by one of them, Henry Ogle.

Shaka quickly realised that the whites could provide some access to goods superior in quality to those he was getting from Delagoa Bay; and he quickly realised the value of firearms in hunting and in raiding his neighbours. But the whites were, to say the least, a disappointment. Fynn wrote early on: 'Only the hope of speedily gained treasure would have induced persons of their character to enter into such a speculation which they were so unfitted for in all its points.' But there was no treasure. What Isaacs later cautiously called 'pecuniary considerations' increasingly embroiled the adventurers in absurd and petty conflict.

For the first three or four years, however, they were to Shaka more interesting than useful, more useful than a nuisance. Squabbling away, they quickly set up separate establishments. Fynn was the most successful. He got involved in Shaka's campaigns early on and was rewarded with cattle, women and permission to set up two establishments, one at isiBubulungu, the second far south on the Mzimkhulu River. Within a year at least one child was conceived to a local wife; within three he had a whole private army.

Farewell built his own so-called Fort Farewell, with a little cannon at each of its four corners, but so unthreatening was the environment that the guns were soon allowed to tip nose-down in the dust. As a naval captain visitor in 1825 noted, they were 'living on the best terms of friendship with the natives and under the protection of the Inguos [*inkosi*] Chaka'.

At first, they weren't much good at feeding themselves, but Shaka kept them going. And when James Saunders King, having lost his first boat at sea, hired the *Mary* and promptly wrecked it on the sandbar, Shaka sent workers to help him build a new one. When John Cane or Charles Rawden Maclean wanted to go to Delagoa Bay, they went with Shaka's blessing and escorts. (They regularly met travellers and hunters or received letters from the Bay: the lines of communication and trade were clearly open.) And when he needed it – as we'll see in more detail in the next chapter – Shaka called on the whites for armed support.

Those campaigns apart, the whites in fact spent very little time with Shaka. But no sooner had they arrived than an attempt was made on Shaka's life. During a night dance at kwaBulawayo, Shaka received an assegai thrust through his left arm and into his ribs. Coughing blood, he was whisked away to receive the attention of his doctors, whose poultices were doubtless more effective than Fynn's camomile tea. (Fynn pretends he was central to the action, but the Zulu sources make no mention of Fynn's presence at all.)

The assegai handle was rounded at one end in the Qwabe fashion. Fynn alleged that revenge attacks were made on some nearby Ndwandwe, and others alleged a massacre of the Qwabe. However, though there seems to have ensued something of a purge of selected Qwabe members, there was no widespread killing. A culprit was caught, his ears cut off and his body dragged out and buried under a huge pile of sticks heaped on him by outraged citizens. But the sources are virtually unanimous: Shaka's half-brothers, Dingane and Mhlangana, were responsible. The attempt had taken place right within the gates of the *isigodlo*: no stray Qwabe would have got anywhere near there.

Did Shaka not suspect his brothers? If he did, could he find no path to eliminating them? Either way, he apparently did nothing. This mysterious omission would prove to be his downfall.

The whites immediately tried to take advantage of the attempt, from which Shaka fairly speedily recovered. Both Fynn and Farewell claimed to have helped Shaka with their medicines. Farewell came away with the prize: an alleged land grant from Shaka. It consisted of a single, obscure, page-long sentence, full of legal jargon, in which Shaka promised Farewell a huge slice of land running a hundred kilometres inland from isiBubulungu, for his and his heirs' sole and uninhibited use 'in perpetuity'. The parchment was signed and countersigned by a whole bunch of people, most of them, black and white alike, illiterate; and it was supported by two codicils which reveal that Farewell's main worry was that Shaka understood clearly what he had done.

The dates on the document are inconsistent, and it's unclear whether it was a 'grant' or a 'sale'. Most importantly, it is inconceivable that Shaka would have understood the deal in the terms Farewell was insisting on: this was not a mode of ownership which Shaka would recognise. It involved land either already under the control of his client-chiefs or outside his range of influence altogether. Any way you look at it, it was a fraud.

It would not be the last. King and Isaacs tried to persuade the Cape government that Shaka had granted them the St Lucia area and the mouth of the Mlazi River. No document ever emerged to support this. Later still, as we'll see in a moment, King tried to fly an alleged land grant while he was in Port Elizabeth, claiming exactly the same area allegedly already given to Farewell – and later still, years after Shaka's death, Fynn made several attempts to convince the colonial government that Shaka had actually ceded it all to *him*.

While the whites tried to depict themselves as having near-mystical powers over Shaka, in fact he treated them entirely pragmatically – when he saw them, which wasn't often. After the first visit in 1825, neither King nor Fynn saw him again for nearly a year. As for Isaacs, by his own account he made only a handful of short visits over four years, together amounting to no more than three or four months. Most of the time, they were trying to steal ivory and slaves from under Shaka's nose, fighting among themselves and busying themselves about their own settlements. By and large, they had found what Farewell called a 'comfortable asylum'. The Zulu historian Magema Fuze, writing in the 1920s, described their situation accurately enough: 'To these white people Shaka gave girls from his [*isigodlo*], who became their wives. They bore them many children, now comprising several clans, and those clans are still known by the names of their fathers. They are distinguishable by being white, but they are black in all other respects.' Fynn habitually wore an *umutsha*, a leather loincloth, when he visited Shaka; it was the dress code, and Fynn conformed.

The whites hedged their bets, though, and maintained their links with the business community at the Cape. King wheedled gunpowder and guns from the Cape government, despite their suspicion of him. At first he pictured Shaka as all but a kindly godfather, and Natal as a delightful place for others to come and settle, but when it suited him he completely changed his tune. By 1827, he was insisting that the frail colony at Port Natal was in terrible 'distress and privations', and Shaka was a monstrous despot slaughtering hundreds every day. It was only because the English public was already familiar with, and receptive to, such savage stereotypes of Africa that King's lies stuck at all.

Despite his increasing irritation, Shaka tried to use the link with the Cape to his advantage. This may have been one factor in his move from kwaBulawayo to kwaDukuza in 1827, though a minor one. Farewell floated the idea that Shaka should – if he could not go himself – send an emissary to the Cape, even to make contact with King George III of England himself, about whom he had heard a great deal.

This idea eventually came to fruition in 1828. The conditions of its birth are murky. King somehow managed to muscle Farewell out, and it was he and Isaacs who took Shaka's emissaries to Port Elizabeth. King finished building his boat (sycophantically named the *Chaka*, but renamed *Elizabeth and Susan* the moment they crossed the sandbar), loaded up a respected if irascible Zulu elder called Sothobe, the former prisoner and now interpreter 'Hlambamanzi', and various attendants, and set sail on 10 March 1828.

In Port Elizabeth, the 'embassy' ran into instant difficulties. It became obvious that King was entirely untrustworthy. The Cape officials couldn't discover what the aims of the mission were at all. King whined, wriggled and threatened to sail back to Natal, but the government refused to register his 'foreign-built' vessel. A heap of ivory, a gift from Shaka to the Governor, disappeared. Sothobe made various attempts to escape to the colonial frontier, then lying some 200 kilometres to the east.

There, a series of convulsions among the peoples of the interior was being attributed solely to Shaka. Marauders, collectively known as 'Fetcanie', were sowing mayhem in spasmodic attacks on the Mpondo and other Xhosa-speaking clans along the lower and upper Mthatha rivers (around the present-day city of Umtata). A military force under Major Dundas discovered serious devastation in western Mpondo country, but Dundas wasn't clear on the culprits. He was joined by Colonel Henry Somerset; together they pursued rumours of another 'Fetcanie' or 'Zulu' force on the upper Mthatha. They went in with artillery, followed up with sabres, and discovered that in fact they had slaughtered the desperate remnants of Matiwane's Ngwane, who had been wandering further west in search of somewhere to settle. The massacre was passed off as the 'battle of Mbolompho'.

Meanwhile, it was learned that the attacks on the lower Mthatha had not been made by the Zulu, either. The Zulu *had* raided the Mpondo again in May 1828, but another force was on the rampage still in June.

The missionary William Shrewsbury, stationed at Butterworth, interviewed refugees and inadvertently revealed the identity of the 'commander': Mbulazi, 'the Killer'. It was Henry Francis Fynn. (As we'll see in the next chapter, he was up to no good.)

It is virtually certain that King, back in Port Elizabeth, knew that this raid was in the offing, and that his main aim was to elicit colonial support for it. He was astounded when this support was not forthcoming. He suddenly produced another apparent land grant from Shaka, which was correctly divined as completely fraudulent. The government washed its hands of the whole thing, packed the embassy onto the naval sloop *Helicon*, and on 7 August set them homeward for Port Natal.

Shaka was incensed at the embassy's failure, at the disappearance of his ivory, and at the paltry gifts he had received in return. King, he fumed, was 'like a monkey', getting his fingers into everything. He expressed commiserations when King, ill on arrival at isiBubulungu, died in late August, but it couldn't have seemed to him much of a loss.

Shaka almost immediately decided to dispatch another embassy, to be led by John Cane, this time overland. By the time Cane and the carefully instructed chiefs sent with him arrived in the Colony, however, events back in Zulu country had overtaken them.

## 10

# Red assegais

*The final phase, 1824–1828*

'Finding themselves face to face with so monstrously conducted and so wholly unjustifiable a series of campaigns, as unconscionable as Germany's submarine policy was for us in the late war, it might well be anticipated, had breathing time or opportunity been afforded, that numbers of more or less connected though theoretically independent tribes would, in the hour of a common supreme danger, have formed powerful confederacies to withstand and possibly turn the tables on [Shaka's] rapidly and, therefore, seemingly insecurely constructed army. Such confederacies were, indeed, arranged, especially in Natal, though nowhere can it be said that they met with success, certainly no success in stemming the onflow of lava from the human volcano ever rumbling and thundering at Bulawayo, plotting new mischief.'

So wrote James Stuart, in 'Tshaka, the Great Zulu Despot', a 1924 piece calculated to appeal to all the old imperialist stereotypes. Yet less than eight years before, this same James Stuart had been compiling his oral records, which, as we've already seen, largely gave a very different picture. Granted, these records had their problems. Mqaikana kaYenge was 85 or 86 when James Stuart had him brought in by train in May 1916. The old man was stooped, darkly bronzed, intelligent and knowledgeable. If anyone could throw light on the complex politics of Shaka's ventures south of the Thukela, Mqaikana could. But even he had his limits. 'I used to listen to old people speaking,' Mqaikana said, 'telling us what they chose, but we did not especially interrogate them, much less commit to paper … I am very sorry indeed I never learned to write.' So it is that only through a haze of half-remembered facts, patchy and tentative, can we approach the tangled events of the period.

But this much should be clear by now: Shaka was not just a 'human volcano' spilling across the countryside, incinerating everyone before him. This is not true even of his final years: the aggressive phase.

Shaka had certainly begun by cobbling together a Zulu-centred polity primarily for defence. He learned to use the methods of offence mostly to gain security – not conquest for its own sake. He was not involved in massacring anybody. He did not have a 'standing army' that needed to be occupied with fighting year-round.

Although there were doubtless a number of smaller cattle raids and tribute-gathering expeditions that have been lost from the record, most of the time Shaka and his people would have been engaged in the more mundane activities of daily life.

By 1824, however, he evidently felt in a position to make some more aggressive, long-distance raids. Whether the stimulus was power-hunger, real hunger caused by droughts, desire for greater wealth or a need for other resources is arguable: probably a different mix of these in each case. The scope of these raids should not be overstated. For the five years 1824 to 1828 inclusive, we know of no more than seven major expeditions – a bit more than once a year during the raiding season when the rivers were passable. Each took no more than a few weeks. Only one can be considered a major battle. Success was patchy.

This period was also punctuated by two other serious internal events: Shaka's move to kwaDukuza and the death of his mother Nandi. We'll look at these as they occur in between the long-distance campaigns.

We've already related the Zulus' first long raid, the failed *amabece* campaign against the Mpondo in early 1824. Their second, about a year later, was much more successful. This raid was on Macingwane of the Chunu, living around present-day Richmond. The attack conforms more readily to the stereotype. This is Mqaikana kaYenge's account: 'Shaka appeared on the scene with his army, ... taking up a position on the Pateni hill [south-west of present-day Richmond] as the army went forward to attack Macingwane. Macingwane, finding he was no match for Shaka, immediately moved off with his stock, women and children across the Mzimkhulu and Ingwagwane [rivers] to a district about Insikeni mountain, where there was a forest [40 kilometres north of present-day Kokstad]. The cattle and children, also the *impi*, took refuge in the forest. Before the mountain was a plain on which the Zulu army was drawn up and where it was given its instructions. Macingwane himself went and took up a position on the very top of a mountain, going to a point, and from there he observed Shaka's tactics. Shaka himself was with his forces – for he never failed to accompany them in person until the occasion of his assassination, when the army was away in the north-east. The Zulus then moved forward and *tshaya*'d *ingomane*, i.e. simultaneously struck their shields loudly, and so loudly that the cattle in the forest became terrified and emerged into the open. This was the signal for closing in. The Zulus entered the forest, fought and defeated the Cunus, killing off even women and children without exception. In the meantime, Macingwane, seeing the game was up, came down the mountain and fled to Pondoland. Thus Shaka got the whole of the Cunu cattle.'

One thing here is wrong: Shaka was not always with his forces. Mqaikana's assertion that women and children were killed 'without exception' also needs qualifying. Macingwane himself disappeared; some Chunu joined footloose 'Fetcanie' marauders who redounded into the Transkei or became refugees – 'Mfengu' – to be absorbed into the Colony's labour pool. Other Chunu, moreover, moved back to join the Zulu themselves or stayed where they were. They were not obliterated.

When James King wrecked the *Mary* at Port Natal, he found that Farewell and others had been off fighting in the interior. It seems likely that the Macingwane raid was the occasion. It would not be long before the whites were involved again. In July 1826, Shaka found it necessary – or found an opportunity – to launch a devastating attack on his old enemies, the Ndwandwe.

As we saw in Chapter 5, the 'Mvuzane fight' had helped shunt Zwide off north but had by no means destroyed the Ndwandwe threat. Zwide's son Sikhunyane had sneered, 'Shaka has overcome you, for you are an old man. He will not overcome my age-grade.' After some minor skirmishes, Shaka took the initiative. Accompanied by Zihlandlo of the Mkhize and others, he called up the whites and marched a large force northwards. Amongst the eZindololwane hills, just north of the Phongolo River, they met Sikhunyane's army.

Accounts of the fight are thin and contradictory. Fynn admitted that white gunmen were engaged: he was rewarded with cattle, the so-called Usuthu beasts. He also exaggeratedly claimed that 40 000 Ndwandwe died; Charles Maclean, who must have been informed by Fynn in the first place, recorded only 3000 Ndwandwe dead, and 1500 cattle captured as against Fynn's 60 000. Not so devastating after all. The Zulu informant Mbokodo kaSekulekile's version is both more detailed and, for anyone hunting for evidence of Shaka's military genius, a little disappointing: 'After being prepared, the troops left, forming two horns, and surrounded that mountain. Before they could surround the mountain, Sikhunyane escaped. Shaka saw him flee. The two horns met and began stabbing one another, for the people, being very numerous, did not know one another. But they soon discovered, and desisted. Sikhunyane himself had escaped, but his *impi* had been hemmed in. "Kill off every soul," said Shaka, "woman and child." He wanted nothing of Sikhunyane's to survive. The *impi* went and finished them all off. Shaka then directed the troops to follow after Sikhunyane, but they failed to overtake him.'

It is said one can still find the bones of the dead soldiers at the foot of eZindololwane's cliffs. Maclean denied a follow-up massacre, though, saying only that the area's crops were razed to 'a barren and desolate wilderness', and in this way the Ndwandwe were 'entirely annihilated'. Possibly some captives were fed into the slave trade, which by this stage was booming. Despite that, there *were* survivors who, Shaka proclaimed, 'should be spared and received as his children, and worthy of becoming the companions of Zulu warriors'. Indeed, adding 'these brave men to his band of warriors' was Shaka's 'primary and only motive'. Nevertheless, it was effectively the end of the independent Ndwandwe.

One might have thought that Shaka would have taken this opportunity to move back north into the Zulu ancestral heartland. Not so. He then moved *south* again, from kwaBulawayo to kwaDukuza (later Stanger). There is no obvious explanation. Some said it was because of the assassination attempt, but this had been two years earlier. The whites said that it was so he could be near *them*, but there was no great advantage to Shaka in this. Probably it was simply a move to utilise still more attractive resources in that area, and use them for an extension of his colonial policy of building clusters of settlements in the vicinity of his 'capital'.

Shaka was not quite finished with the north. In 1827 he called up white gunmen again, this time for a minor punitive expedition (the fourth of the seven) against a recalcitrant segment of the Khumalo, the Bheje. The Bheje were holed up in a mountainous redoubt; gunfire helped dislodge them where assegais couldn't. Nathaniel Isaacs got a barb in his bottom; Shaka joked he should be killed for cowardice, for he had obviously been running away. He rewarded him and his sailor companions with women and cattle anyway.

In the same year – unusually – a fifth expedition went out. It was unusual in a number of ways and came to be known as 'the *impi* of wrongdoing'. It was apparently led by Dingane (about whose activities throughout Shaka's reign we know next to nothing). It did not have Shaka's blessing; it was not ritually doctored before departure. It was a madcap, astonishingly long raid against Matiwane of the Ngwane, who had by now moved even further away across the Drakensberg and into the Caledon River valley, north of present-day Lesotho. They did catch up with Matiwane; they fought each other to a standstill; Dingane got wounded; they came back with little to show for their effort. This illicit raid was not a success.

Shortly afterwards, the second domestic event of note happened: Nandi died, in August 1827. This has also been hugely exaggerated in importance (mostly, not surprisingly, by Fynn). Shaka, it would be said, went crazy with grief. Fynn was right about one thing, though: Nandi died of natural causes – not because Shaka himself murdered her for hiding an unwanted child of his. This was surely a slander put about by Shaka's detractors later.

Nor was there a vast wave of insane violence resulting from Nandi's demise. In his earliest account, Fynn numbered no more than about a dozen actual opportunistic killings: as soon as Shaka heard about them, he put a stop to it. (Fynn much later pumped this up to 7000 dead, a wholly invented figure that has continued to dominate the literature.) No doubt a few vendettas were worked off, but the stories of people being slaughtered (including, in some overheated accounts, the 'whole Qwabe nation') for failing to mourn, or for pretending to do so by putting spittle or snuff in the corners of their eyes, are nonsense.

Nor did the mourning continue for a whole year, inducing mass starvation, killing of pregnant women and the rest of the popular fiction. As even Isaacs makes clear, the mourning went on for a single judicious month, one 'moon'; Shaka then went into the forest for a ritual purification, after which routines returned to normal. Nandi was buried near kwaBulawayo, where you can still visit her grave, a sadly neglected plinth in an overgrown field.

Only one mourning ritual remained: a cleansing or *ihlambo* campaign. It took more than a year to mature. The *ihlambo* expedition, it was decided, would be against the Mpondo; it would compensate for the humiliation of the *amabece* campaign. The army left kwaDukuza at much the same time as the ill-fated 'embassy' under James Saunders King sailed for Port Elizabeth. Shaka accompanied his army part of the way. He took several *amabutho*, including a unit of girls, the uNkisimana, who had been recently *buthwa*'d – called up – at kwaDukuza. Shaka crossed the Mzimkhulu and halted, taking up a position at or near Fynn's *umuzi*, protected by the Fasimba, while the main body advanced. Faku and the Mpondo apparently chose not to fight but retreated towards the Drakensberg, leaving the Zulu forces to rustle their cattle at will. Only one account implies that there was a clash, and that not a serious one. The raid caused minimal damage and never went anywhere near the colonial frontier. As Major Dundas found when he arrived in Faku's country in late July 1828, Shaka's forces had long withdrawn – but Henry Francis Fynn had been there more recently, and with far more devastating results.

Fynn later concocted a long story about how he had *actually* been travelling back with Shaka as a 'hostage', arguing him out of being nasty and teaching him how to bake pancakes. Fynn deliberately omitted the most dramatic event of the whole expedition. Was he concealing his own complicity? For it was not far from

Fynn's *umuzi* that Shaka, whilst heading for home, paused on a flat rock beside the Mkhomazi river. His half-brothers Dingane and Mhlangana and others were with him. The main *impi* was busy crossing further upstream. Dingane and Mhlangana, and possibly Mbopha, Shaka's personal assistant, closed in on him, pretending to kneel in supplication but intent in fact on assassinating him then and there. Fortunately for Shaka, they were interrupted. A man named Lucunge chanced by. Seeing Shaka there, he tried hastily to withdraw, but Shaka spotted him and summoned him over. Lucunge knelt. Shaka then ordered those present to 'sharpen' their assegais on Lucunge's forehead as if it were a grindstone. Blood flowed. Lucunge continued to praise Shaka. He was then released, having unwittingly saved the Zulu chief's life.

Once back at kwaDukuza, Shaka then launched the seventh and last raid of these closing years. Totally aberrantly, he sent the army off again almost immediately, leaving himself with no protection. The army was sent to attack Soshangane, now living way north of Delagoa Bay, near present-day Kruger Park, but were annihilated by disease. Or so the story would go.

The Zulu sources, though fragmentary, depict something different. Shaka was not crazy; he was desperate. The region was being devastated by drought; in some ways, drought hit centralised, strongly stratified polities harder than the old, little, scattered ones. The *ihlambo* expedition had not yielded as many cattle as had been hoped. Moreover, it was grain that was more badly needed. Shaka sent out not one but several foraging forays.

The one that was best remembered, however, was a disaster. This was the so-called Bhalule campaign, the 'expedition of far-away', otherwise called the *ukhukhulela ngoqo* – 'sweep-up-the-rubbish', as even the old men with rickety knees were ordered to go. It seems that the Bhalule *impi* swung north and east past the Drakensberg, and got roughed up by a Swazi contingent which opportunistically trapped them against a flooded river (possibly the Phongolo). The remnant then moved further east to the Maphutha River, south of Delagoa Bay, intending to raid Machakhane, a Matoll chieftain then growing in importance, not least through slaving. Learning that he was likely to be bolstered by Portuguese firearms, however, the Zulu backed off. Already depleted, they succumbed on their way home to accidental poisoning from toxic woodsmoke, or to malaria, or to some form of dysentery. They straggled home in small and limping groups, to discover that events back at kwaDukuza had run away without them.

Of Shaka's seven known long-distance campaigns, then, three were successful, one only partly so; one was both illegal and fruitless; and two were outright disasters. A mixed record.

The Bhalule expedition had scarcely left when Shaka got the first hint of trouble: Dingane and Mhlangana, supposedly with the troops, unexpectedly turned up at kwaDukuza. 'Hau! have you returned?' Shaka exclaimed. Ominously, the brothers did not reply.

There is little clarity on what happened next; it's in the nature of conspiracies, of course, that little is ever revealed. Clearly, plotting had been afoot for some time: we have already seen two assassination attempts, both, according to all credible sources, originating with Dingane and Mhlangana. Why Shaka had done nothing to neutralise this threat earlier must remain one of the enduring mysteries of his reign. Dingane, of course, later put it about that he was saving the nation from Shaka's brutality and madness, but as we've seen, there was little of that in fact. Maclean, more plausibly, claimed that Shaka had deliberately refused to marry or acknowledge offspring, having come to an agreement that Dingane would succeed him. Dingane just got impatient. But we don't really know.

We're not even certain about the date and timing. No eyewitnesses survived. Isaacs said the assassination happened on the night of 22 September; Farewell that it was the next day; and Fynn remembered 24 September – the date usually cited although, in fact, it's the least probable. Fynn put together the most detailed account we have, though one can't vouch for its accuracy. 'In the middle of the day on which he was killed being the 24th Septr 1828 he dreamed that he was ded and Umbopo was serving another king on waking he told his dream to one of his Sisters who ... afterwards told Umbopo the circumstance who knowing that in consequence he would not have many hours to live urged the two confederates [Dingane and Mhlangana] to take the first opportunity which shortly occurred when some Caffers arriving from the outskirts of the nation with Cranes feathers which the king had sent them for in which they had delayed much time Chaka came out of his Hut and went to a small krall about 50 yards from Dugusar called Inyarka moobie [iNyakamubhi] where these people that brought the feathers sat before him.'

Fynn's notebook fades to illegibility for a few lines, but if we follow James Stuart's transcription of it, Shaka demanded in 'a severe voice' what had delayed them. Mbopha then uncharacteristically did the same, brandishing a stick. The visitors fled. 'Chaka se[e]ing them run asked Umbopo what they had done to be driven away Umhlengana & Dingarn having hid themselves at the back of the small fence ... standing having an hidden assegai under the kaross se[e]ing the people run and the king by himself stabbed him throu the back by the left shoulder Dingarn ... also stabbed him Chaka having only time to ask what is the matter, children of my father but the three together stabbed him.'

The role of the 'visitors' is particularly suggestive. Almost certainly they were dissident factions of the Mpondo, under Myeki of the Jali and Fodo of the Nhlangwini. Even more interestingly, Myeki and Fodo were both connected with Fynn, at or near whose *umuzi* the previous attempt had been made. Fodo – short, bewhiskered and combative – was known as the leader of a predatory outfit, the first, according to one source, 'to be an *imfacane*, an *impi* that goes along with its women and children in a fighting manner'. Fodo and the Nhlangwini became the core of the Fynn family's iziNkumbi raiders – the Locusts. They were also known as the 'people of Vundlase', Vundlase being Fynn's 'great wife'.

So, though the case remains circumstantial, it appears that Dingane and Mhlangana connived with dissident elements of the Mpondo, Fynn's iziNkumbi and some remnants of the disbanded and disgruntled iziYendane *ibutho*, to bring Shaka down.

Shaka's body was left where it had fallen overnight. Later he was buried, in the customary position, curled upright, in a pit in the middle of that same cattle enclosure, iNyakamubhi. You can still visit the spot today, on a slope in the middle of the town of Stanger, recently renamed kwaDukuza once again.

A T Bryant, a hundred years later, penned what had become the common view of the Zulu founder's death: 'the monster of a myriad crimes rolled over in the dust and gave up his ghost to Satan'. Few Zulu people then, and not many now, would go with that. Shaka was infinitely more complex a man, and equally complex has been his legacy.

## 11

# Aftermaths

Some time during Mpande's reign in the 1840s the royal *umuzi* of Nodwengu was convulsed by the unusual spectacle of two snakes – one marked like a python, the other green and white – writhing in battle along the fences. It was immediately interpreted as the returned spirits, the *amadlozi*, of Dingane and Shaka, fighting each other after death, just as they had in life. 'These kings, Dingane and Shaka, fought each other; they chased each other up and down the fence at the door of Masipula's hut, and finally dropped onto the ground in the yard. They began as the sun was getting warm, and continued until midday. They twined round each other, with first one on top and then the other. They were red with blood from biting each other … The *izinduna* were trying to intervene in the fight, calling out, "Our pardon, kings! What is happening?" Then Mpande's order arrived, "Drive off that evil-doer of Mgungundhlovu [Dingane]. So he is fighting with Shaka when it was he who finished off the sons of Senzangakhona? He used to say that he had killed Shaka for troubling the people; in fact it was he who finished off the Zulu house." … From this we saw that Dingane had spoken with two tongues; [it was Dingane who] had ordered the house of Senzangakhona to be killed off for the vultures, for they were hungry.'

In the end, the 'Dingane' snake was merely caught, defanged and released. It's a fascinating episode, revealing at once the depth and intensity of Zulu beliefs in the presence of their ancestors, the centrality of the leaders to their well-being, and the prevalent opinion about the relative merits of Shaka and his fratricidal successor. It could as easily have been Dingane and his supporters, rather than the white invaders, who were the 'locusts' or 'swallows' Shaka allegedly foresaw taking over the land in his famous (but apocryphal) 'dying prophecy'.

Immediately after Shaka fell, a period of confusion ensued. The debate about the succession took time. Mhlangana was said to have jumped over Shaka's dead body, as a sign that he considered himself the successor. On the other hand, Shaka had given Dingane considerable power over an area north of the Thukela, apparently favouring *him*. Rightly or wrongly, it was decided that Mhlangana had lost his claim, as he had done the killing. He could 'not rule with a red assegai'.

Dingane, ostensibly, was clean. Others claimed that neither Dingane nor Mhlangana was Shaka's own heir designate: the heir was Ngwadi, another half-brother and Nandi's son. Dingane moved swiftly against him. Ngwadi put up a fierce fight, but he and his people were wiped out, perhaps 2000 of them.

Both Mbopha and Mhlangana would shortly be killed off in turn. Over the coming months and even years, Dingane dispatched every one of Shaka's other brothers, with the exception of Mpande. Several of Shaka's client-chieftains were shortly attacked, killed and replaced by Dingane's appointees, alongside dozens of lesser Shakan supporters. If anyone had a 'red assegai', it was Dingane.

Dingane ruled the Zulu people for a round dozen years. He became most infamous, of course, for slaughtering Piet Retief and his party, and for losing to the Boers at the battle of Blood (Ncome) River in 1838. This has obscured the complexities of his internal politics. Though he set about relaxing some of Shaka's marriage restrictions, he retained the essentials of the structures Shaka had founded: the *isigodlo*, the *amabutho*, the *izinduna*. He continued the pattern of raiding widely for cattle: indeed, even more aggressively. He even attacked and wrecked Delagoa Bay in 1833, in aggressive pursuit of trade and slaving opportunities. He was not entirely successful.

He was least successful in retaining the loyalty of his own remaining brother, Mpande. Mpande had always had leg trouble, a protruding bone; this and an appearance of stupidity, perhaps, saved him. He was seen to be politically innocuous. He had the last laugh there: Dingane's reign unravelled entirely when Mpande absconded with 17 000 followers to make a compact with the Boers, finally ousting his brother in a pitched battle on the Thukela in 1839. Dingane fled north across the Phongolo with a few faithfuls, dying miserably very far from home. This was the melancholy climax of the civil war that followed Shaka's assassination.

Mpande went on to rule the Zulu for another thirty-two years, and it was he, more than any other leader, perhaps, who truly cemented Shaka's legacy. It was the culmination of this work that the British faced, initially disastrously, in battles at Isandhlwana and elsewhere in the 1879 invasion of Zululand. Ever since, the reputation of the Zulu as the massed warriors of that war has totally dominated the study of Zulu history. The earlier periods remain severely neglected. There are, for instance, something like twenty biographies of Cecil John Rhodes in existence – some good, some terrible; some pandering, some savagely critical – all competing for attention. The same should be the case with Shaka. Nor do we have a single scholarly biography of either Dingane or Mpande, despite the abundance of material evidence. The picture of the massed Zulu *impi* has become almost synonymous with Zulu national identity, with tragic results. The reality has always been much more complicated.

Shaka had certainly built up a substantial polity and colonised considerable territory. He had gone quite some way towards centralising rituals, an elitist military ethic, trade patterns, and even ways of speaking and thinking. A new identity, or set of identities, was certainly in the process of being forged, centred on the Zulu 'royal' family. Shaka had built up a large and loyal following.

But the so-called Zulu state was not solidly unified – not even within Shaka's family. The scuffles and murders that followed his assassination merely presaged the eruptions of civil war into which the 'nation' fell repeatedly thereafter. It collapsed into civil war after the 1879 war, and again after the last major Zulu rebellion in 1906. Among the many divisions was the divide between fighters and pacifists: the idea that 'the Zulu' are somehow congenitally aggressive warriors does not match all the facts.

The kinds of division within the 'Zulu' polity have also shifted over the years. Today in KwaZulu-Natal, the political divide between Inkatha and ANC supporters dominates, with the former all but a

The late Mazisi Kunene's 430-page poem, published in both English and Zulu, incorporated Zulu- and settler-derived stories and information, in extended izibongo or praise-poem style. It gave Shaka's life nuanced if fictionalised texture, but blew his stature up to almost absurd proportions – and ironically used the abusive and ungrateful Nathaniel Isaacs's inaccurate depiction of Shaka on its cover.

spent force. The kingship itself remains, symbolically, extremely powerful but seems politically more shaky than at any other time in its past. Also, fascinatingly, in the last few years, the leaders of the Ngwane, Hlubi and other peoples have reasserted their claim to be regarded as 'kings' on the same level as the Zulu king, Zwelithini. They are, they claim, just as ancient and illustrious. These identities were not obliterated or wholly assimilated into the 'Zulu nation', by Shaka or anyone since.

As for Shaka himself, his image has varied as often as the spelling of his name. Only in the 1950s, as political opinions changed, would the heroic image – the giant-killer, the military genius – overtake the image of the degenerate, genocidal maniac. In Mazisi Kunene's Zulu epic poem, he becomes *Emperor Shaka the Great*. In 2010 a statue of Shaka, cast in bronze for the entrance of the new King Shaka international airport near Durban, had to be removed because Zulu royalty objected that it made him look 'like a herdboy'. The sculptor's deliberate attempt to transcend the symbolism of heroic militarism was scotched.

So the juggernaut of the mythology slouches on, being continually reborn in the most bizarre forms. One of my favourites is a book entitled *Leadership Lessons from Emperor Shaka the Great* by Phinda Mzwakhe Madi. This is a strange but canny mix of old-

*The sculptor Andries Botha's striking bronze of Shaka, temporarily erected at Durban's King Shaka International Airport, shows the king as more grizzled and wise than most depictions. Botha attempted to transcend the Zulus' reputation for unbridled militarism by placing Shaka between two mythic cattle, his assegai and shield resting on the 'isihlalo' (traditional pillow) nearby. (Photograph by Sean Laurenz, courtesy of Andries Botha)*

man 'oral tradition' and management manual, which purports to derive sound business principles from all the hoary tales of Shaka's derring-do. (Extracts are now available on the internet, posted to help 'strengthen the Virtual Black Community today'.) But importantly, the 'new history' not only tries to dismiss such 'mythology' in order to arrive at a single 'historical truth'; it also recognises that the myths become themselves part of history, part of the way people identify themselves, part of their motivations for very real behaviour. It also recognises that the construction of the 'truth' is always a textual, literary and therefore provisional and arguable exercise.

Nevertheless, Shaka has needed to be rescued from the obvious lies and distortions. He was not superhuman. We should instead view him realistically, within real contexts, as the canny politician, the opportunist, the make-do artist, a tough, complex and able man who was gifted and limited in the ways all leaders are. Much more work remains to be done, especially on environmental and economic conditions, on family relationships and marital patterns, on individual leaders and the separate peoples. We have made only a beginning.

# Further reading

Carton, Ben, John Laband and Jabulani Sithole (eds.), *Zulu Identities: Being Zulu, Past and Present*. University of KwaZulu-Natal Press, Pietermaritzburg, 2008

Cobbing, Julian, 'The Mfecane as Alibi: Thoughts on Dithakong and Mbolompo', *Journal of African History* 29, 1988, 487–519

Duminy, Andrew and Bill Guest (eds.), *Natal and Zululand: From Earliest Times to 1910. A New History*. University of Natal Press, Pietermaritzburg, 1989

Etherington, Norman, *The Great Treks: The Transformation of Southern Africa, 1815–1854*. Pearson Education, Harlow, 2001

Gray, Stephen (ed.), *The Natal Papers of 'John Ross' [Charles Rawden Maclean]*. University of Natal Press, Pietermaritzburg, 1992

Hamilton, Carolyn (ed.), *The Mfecane Aftermath: Reconstructive Debates in Southern African History.* Wits University Press, Johannesburg, 1995

Hamilton, Carolyn, *Terrific Majesty: The Powers of Shaka Zulu and the Limits of Historical Invention.* David Philip, Cape Town, 1998

Smith, AK, 'Delagoa Bay and the Trade of South-East Africa' in R Gray and D Birmingham (eds.), *Pre-colonial African Trade*. Oxford University Press, Oxford, 1970

Whitelaw, Gavin, 'Preliminary Results of a Survey of Bulawayo, Shaka kaSenzangakhona's Capital', *Southern African Field Archaeology* 3, 1994, 107–9

Wright, JB and A Manson, 1983. *The Hlubi Chiefdom in Zululand-Natal: A History*. Ladysmith Historical Society, Ladysmith, 1993

Wright, JB and C de B Webb (eds.), *The James Stuart Archive*, 5 vols. University of Natal Press, Pietermaritzburg, 1976–2001

Wright, John, 'Rediscovering the Ndwandwe' in Natalie Swanepoel, Amanda Esterhuysen and Philip Bonner (eds.), *Five Hundred Years Rediscovered*. Wits University Press, Johannesburg, 2008

Wylie, Dan, *Savage Delight: White Myths of Shaka*. University of Natal Press, Pietermaritzburg, 2000

Wylie, Dan, *Myth of Iron: Shaka in History*. University of KwaZulu-Natal Press, Pietermaritzburg, 2006

# Index

Bheje (Khumalo) 129
Bryant, AT 21–2, 40, 43, 49, 82, 137
kwaBulawayo 73, 79, 109, 115, 128
Buthelezi 41
Cane, John 16, 115, 121
Cele (Magaye) 75, 90, 93
Cele, Henry 7–8
Chunu (Macingwane) 36, 71, 76, 124–6
circumcision 37, 45
Cobbing, Julian 34
Dingane kaSenzangakhona 40, 58, 67, 97, 101–2, 116, 129, 131–6, 138–41
Dundas, Major Henry 120, 131
Du Preez, Max 9–10
Dube (Khutshwayo) 77
kwaDukuza 119, 128, 131, 134
Farewell, Francis 16, 23, 27, 76–7, 111–12, 116–19, 126, 134
Fuze, Magema 118
Fynn, Henry Francis 15–17, 19–21, 62, 95–6, 105, 111–21, 127, 130–2, 134–6

genealogies 33, 45–7, 89–90
Gluckman, Max 101
Hall, Martin 83
Hamilton, Carolyn 50, 89–90
Hlubi 36, 61, 76, 144; (iziYendane) 78–9, 136
Isaacs, Nathaniel 10–12, 15, 18–19, 74, 77, 81, 106, 114, 129
*isigodlo* 37, 49, 73, 79, 86–8, 90, 116, 118, 140
*ithakazelo* (praise-names) 92–3
Jacob Msimbithi 113–14, 119
Jama 42
Kay, Stephen 17, 100
Khomfiya 70–1
Khumalo (Mzilikazi) 9, 109, 129
King, James Saunders 10, 16–18, 45, 111–21, 126
Kunene, Mazisi 143–4
Langazana 92
Langeni 46–8, 51–2, 57, 71
Leslie, David 56
Maclean, Charles Rawden 23–4, 46, 87–8, 99–101, 107, 115, 127, 134

153

Makhedama (see also Langeni) 51–2
Maphitha 67, 75
marital organisation 85–9
Mbolompho (battle) 120
Mbopha 100, 135–6, 140
Mbovu kaMtshumayeli 25
'mfecane' 28–36
Mfengu 126
Mhlangana 116, 132, 134–6, 139–40
militarisation and military organisation 33–6, 42–3, 59–60, 73–4, 82–3, 90, 123; *amabutho* 37, 49, 52, 65, 72–3, 76, 83, 94, 131, 140; *amakhanda* 73–4, 83, 92; *izinduna* 37, 49, 77, 82, 90–94, 140
Mkhize (Zihlandlo) 37, 71, 74–6, 126
Mnkabayi 43, 57, 92
Morris, Donald 82, 101
Mpande kaSenzangakhona 138–9, 141–2
Mpondo (Faku) 109–11, 120–1, 124, 131
Mqaikana kaYenge 25, 123, 125
Mthethwa (Dingiswayo) 36–7, 42, 48–60, 62–3, 78, 100, 110
Mudli 40, 54, 58
Mzilikazi (see also Khumalo) 66–8
Nandi 39–47, 129–30, 140
Ndhlovu kaThimuni 39–41, 46, 54, 59
Ndwandwe (Zwide) 36–7, 49, 59–67, 68–73, 75, 109, 116, 126–8
Ngomane kaMqomboli 52

Ngwane (Matiwane) 61, 66, 129, 144
Nhlangwini (Fodo) 136
Ntshalini 60
Ogle, Henry 114
Omer-Cooper, John 28
Owen, WFW 31, 111
Phakathwayo (see also Qwabe) 72
Philipps, Thomas 27–28
Qwabe (Nqetho) 37, 57, 61–4, 71–3, 110, 116, 130
Ritter, EA 9–10, 22–3, 40, 65
Senghor, Léopold 9
Senzangakhona 39–48, 51, 54–7
Shaka kaSenzangakhona: myths about, 7–13, 27–9, 82, 122–3, 130, 144–6; sources on 14–26; birth 39, 44–6; naming of 40, 47, 53; childhood 46–8; under Mthethwa 48–57, 60; takes over Zulu 54–9; and Ndwandwe 59–67, 69, 126–8; 'Mvuzane fight' 63–6; military tactics 61–4, 76–8, 127–8; and client-chiefs 62, 67, 74–9; and Qwabe 69–74; domestic organisation 86–90; propaganda and language 93–4; *hlonipha* 94; brutality 94–105; appearance 97; sexuality and marriage 53–4, 101; generosity 105–8; and whites 109–20; last campaigns 110–12, 124–33; first assassination attempt 115–16; and land grants 15, 117, 121; and Nandi's death

154

129–30; second assassination attempt 131–2; and Bhalule campaign 133–4; death 134–7; legacy 138–46
*Shaka Zulu* 7–8
Shepstone, Theophilus 21
Shoshangane (Jere) 66, 132
Shrewsbury, William 121
Sigujana 51, 56–8
Sikhunyane (see also Ndwandwe) 126–7
Sithole (Jobe) 71, 75
slavery 30–1, 34–8, 118
Somerset, Henry 120
Stuart, James 24–5, 39, 101, 105, 122–3
Thembu (Ngoza) 36, 57, 71, 76
Thuli (Mathubane) 75, 101
trade 29–31, 35–6, 66, 114
*umkhosi* (first fruits ceremony) 37, 88
Wright, John 22, 36
Zibizendhlela kaShaka 54
Zulu: origins 40–2; nature of state 81–94, 142
Zwangendaba (Gaza) 36, 66